10-2-75

The
Economics
and Politics
of the
Middle East

THE MIDDLE EAST
Economic and Political Problems and Prospects

Studies from a research program of
The Rand Corporation
and
Resources for the Future, Inc.
Sidney S. Alexander, *Program Director*

PUBLISHED

Marion Clawson, Hans H. Landsberg, *and* Lyle T. Alexander
The Agricultural Potential of the Middle East

Sam H. Schurr *and* Paul T. Homan
with Joel Darmstadter, Helmut Frank, John J. Schanz, Jr.,
Thomas R. Stauffer, *and* Henry Steele
Middle Eastern Oil and the Western World: Prospects and Problems

Charles A. Cooper *and* Sidney S. Alexander *(eds.)*
Economic Development and Population Growth in the Middle East

Paul Y. Hammond *and* Sidney S. Alexander *(eds.)*
Political Dynamics in the Middle East

Abraham S. Becker, Bent Hansen, *and* Malcolm H. Kerr
with a Foreword by S.S. Alexander
The Economics and Politics of the Middle East

The Economics and Politics of the Middle East

Abraham S. Becker

Bent Hansen

Malcolm H. Kerr

Foreword by
SIDNEY S. ALEXANDER

American Elsevier Publishing Company, Inc.
New York · London · Amsterdam

AMERICAN ELSEVIER PUBLISHING COMPANY, INC.
52 Vanderbilt Avenue, New York, N.Y. 10017

ELSEVIER PUBLISHING COMPANY
335 Jan Van Galenstraat, P.O. Box 211
Amsterdam, The Netherlands

International Standard Book Number 0-444-00149-2

Library of Congress Card Number 74-14466

Library of Congress Cataloging in Publication Data

Becker, Abraham Samuel, 1927-
   The economics and politics of the Middle East.
   (The Middle East economic and political problems and
prospects)
   Includes indexes.
   1. Near East–Economic conditions. 2. Near East–
Politics and government. 3. Near East–Foreign rela-
tions. I. Hansen, Bent, 1920-   II. Kerr,
Malcolm H. III. Title.
HC410.7.B36   330.9'56'04   74-14466
ISBN 0-444-00150-6

Manufactured in the United States of America

1882984

Contents

Contributing Authors

Abraham S. Becker
Senior Economist, The Rand Corporation,
Santa Monica, California

Bent Hansen
Professor of Economics, University of
California, Berkeley, California

Malcolm H. Kerr
Professor of Political Science, University
of California, Los Angeles, California

Foreword by
Sidney S. Alexander
Professor of Economics and Management,
Sloan School of Management, Massachusetts
Institute of Technology, Cambridge, Mass.;
Director of Research, The Rand-Resources
for the Future Middle East Research Project

Foreword

The studies in this volume are offered to bring up to date, and indeed to amplify, some of the principal findings of a broad program of research on the economics and politics of the Middle East, supported by a grant from the Ford Foundation and carried forward jointly by the Rand Corporation and Resources for the Future, Inc., under my general direction. Studies of three topics deemed particularly worthy of updating and amplification were commissioned for this volume:

1. The developmental prospects on the eve of the 1973 war, covered by Professor Bent Hansen of the University of California at Berkeley.

2. The political outlook in the local area, discussed by Professor Malcolm Kerr of the University of California at Los Angeles.

3. The role of the United States and the USSR in the Middle East conflict, explored by Dr. Abraham Becker of the Rand Corporation.

The previously published economic studies were based upon an assumption of an early peace. That assumption was made, not as the most probable expectation, but rather because it posed the interesting problem: What would the developmental prospects of these countries be if peace could be attained? Professor Hansen's study in this volume reviews the other side of the coin—what development was possible during the years of war and cease-fire. Now, in 1974, it is once again appropriate to ask what sort of economic development would be possible under conditions of peace. Not that peace has yet been attained, but the prospects look better now than they ever have in the past. Egypt, in particular, seems to be orienting its governmental apparatus toward an emphasis upon economic development rather than on war-making.

The 1973 war has wrought a great change in the Middle East situation, bringing into operation some important but previously latent forces. What was needed in the Middle East was a war that was won by both parties, and the 1973 war seems to fill this paradoxical specification. The Arabs have demonstrated their ability to fight effectively and so have restored that dignity which is their primary need. And the Israeli leadership, though militarily victorious, has been driven to a new, and rather grim, realization of Israel's situation. Most of the standard Israeli perceptions of its situation have been demonstrated to be no longer valid—if ever they were. The Arab social system cannot be depended upon to keep the Arabs from fighting effectively. Nor can technological backwardness preclude skillful use of Arab military equipment. The limits of Israel's independence of the United States were demonstrated when, as Dayan said, the shells we shoot in the afternoon were delivered just that morning. So the third way between real peace and the *status quo*, long dismissed by Israel's leadership, has now become the path that must be trod. That third way involves the shift from reliance on occupation of the conquered territories for military security to the use of alternatives such as demilitarization, United Nations' buffer forces, and superpower guarantees. Whether such arrangements offer as much security as did occupation of the territories is beside the point, since indefinitely continued occupation no longer seems a realistic option. Unfortunately, the body politic of Israel is unprepared for this change of circumstances; even as this new direction becomes imperative for Israel, political support is shifting toward "hard-liners," whose policies, it seems to me, would be lethal for Israel in the current situation. Not only did the 1973 war demonstrate Israel's dependence on the United States, but the Arab oil cutback exercised powerful Arab leverage on the United States, principally through Western Europe and Japan. In these circumstances it is to be feared that Israel may find herself in a role previously played by the Arabs—that of being ready to grant concessions only when they are too late. There may still be time for a satisfactory settlement, but not very much remains. Concessions that would be welcome now may later seem inadequate.

It does seem possible at this moment that peace is attainable. Not a perfect peace, perhaps, but one that will permit the tides of passion to ebb. In particular, it is possible that Egypt's preoccupation with the problem of Israel can now be removed, thus permitting her to direct her efforts toward economic development. That same arrangement might relieve Israel of her preoccupation with security, simply by reducing her insecurity.

These are not idle dreams, but realistic possibilities. What shape such a settlement must take I have already outlined in my Foreword to an earlier volume.[1] The one feature of such a settlement which is still problematic is whether Russia is prepared to accept a peaceful outcome. There is enough of a victory for the USSR in that outcome, and enough participation in achieving it, to furnish at least the possibility of her acquiescence. As for the other parties, Egypt has everything to gain, Israel can probably do much better now than later, and the United States can come out a hero. It is hard to conceive of a better opportunity in a situation so amply cursed with inconsistent aspirations.

Should it fail—and there are plenty of chances for it to fail—there will be a

[1] Paul J. Hammond and Sidney S. Alexander, eds., *Political Dynamics in the Middle East,* (New York: American Elsevier, 1972), pp. xxviii–ix.

choice only among catastrophes. It is this mixed prospect, then, to which these studies furnish the background.

Sidney S. Alexander

Cambridge, Massachusetts

PART I

Middle East Development Prospects– What they look like in 1973

Bent Hansen

PART I

Middle East Development Prospects—What They Look Like in 1973

Bent Hansen

The studies on economic development in the Middle Eastern countries, published in an earlier volume in this research program,[1] were all written in or before 1970, and were based upon assumptions that today appear not only optimistic but entirely unrealistic. In particular, the authors assumed that the hostilities between Arab countries and Israel would cease, and Israeli occupation of Arab land would largely be reversed in the near future. This assumption has not proved correct. The years of uncertain cease-fire that have passed since then have already had lasting consequences for development in the countries most directly involved in the conflict, especially those on the Arab side—Egypt, Jordan, and Syria.[2] On the other hand, partly unexpected developments have taken place during the last few years in the oil markets and in the position of the rich Arab oil countries which potentially improve the development perspectives of the Arab world. In addition, these developments have had repercussions on the Great Power policies in the area. The tendency to expansion of the European Economic Community (EEC) and its possible extension of favored treatment to Mediterranean countries is another factor that may favorably change the economic prospects of the area. Thus, there are a number of reasons that call for a reconsideration of the projections made in the above-mentioned studies.

The writing of Part I was completed in September 1973, before the outbreak of the October 1973 war. The author has added a few notes in March 1974 at points where later developments have made the text obsolete.

[1] Charles A. Cooper and Sidney S. Alexander, eds., *Economic Development and Population Growth in the Middle East,* (New York: American Elsevier, 1972).

[2] By calling these countries "directly involved" I mean, not only that they took part in the June 1967 War, but also that they keep a large military machine ready for eventual future acts of war. In neither sense is Lebanon directly involved, although it is a main base of Palestinian guerillas and has been harassed by Israeli raids; economically, these circumstances have been of minor consequence for Lebanon, however.

I. Growth During the Years of War and Cease-fire

National product and income data are inadequate in most of the countries of the Middle East. Only for Egypt and Israel is it possible to quantify economic growth with some degree of accuracy. Their growth rates since 1965 are set out in Table 1. The overall picture is remarkably similar for these two countries, but that is partly coincidental. After a period of high growth rates, ending in 1965, both countries experienced two years of an almost stagnant Gross National Product (GNP) and declining per capita income. The economic stagnation of both countries was the consequence of poor demand management policies during the first half of the sixties: To curb inflation and stabilize the economy both Egypt and Israel found it necessary to put on the brakes and stop development for some time. From 1968 on, policies were again expansionistic in both countries. Israel reached very high growth rates in 1968 and 1969, largely recovering after the recession and settling down thereafter at what, for that country, must be considered a relatively modest growth rate of about 8 percent, somewhat less than the average of 9.1–10.0 percent of 1960–1965 (see Table 1).

Table 1

Growth Rates in Egypt and Israel
(Percentages)

Year	Egypt* (GDP at Constant 1964 Purchasers' Values)	Israel (GDP at Constant 1964 Purchasers' Values)
1960–1965, average	5.5	9.1 –10.00
1965	5.0	9.1
1966	–0.3	1.1
1967	–0.8	2.2
1968	5.5	14.9
1969	8.2)) 5.8	12.3
1970	3.4)	7.7
1971	4.0	8.1

*Year indicates beginning of budget year 1 July–30 June.
  Sources: Egypt–Central Department of Mobilization and Statistics, Cairo; Bent Hansen, "Economic Development of Egypt," in *Economic Development and Population Growth in the Middle East,* ed. Charles A. Cooper and Sidney S. Alexander (New York: American Elsevier, 1972). Israel–*Statistical Abstract of Israel,* 1972; A.L. Gaathon, *Economic Productivity in Israel,* (New York: Bank of Israel and Praeger, 1971), p. 4.

For Egypt the growth rates were influenced by crop fluctuations, but, on balance, the post-June 1967 war growth rate has been about 5 percent; that is, somewhat less than for the period of 1960–1965. Population growth in Israel declined, however, during the sixties. For Israel, the annual growth rate of per capita income seems to have been about the same in the years around 1970[3] as it was during the first half of the sixties while for Egypt it has been somewhat lower: about 2 percent in Egypt as compared with about 5 percent in Israel.

It would be a great mistake to conclude from these per capita growth figures that so far as development is concerned, everything is back to normal, and that the war has had little consequence for developmental prospects. While this, as we shall see, may be approximately true for Israel, it is certainly not the case for Egypt and the other directly involved Arab countries.

First, Egypt has not made up for her growth loss during 1966–1967. Full recovery in Egypt would have required growth rates around 11 percent in 1968–1969, instead of the average of less than 6 percent actually achieved; compare with the very high growth rates in Israel for 1968–1969 which compensated for the slow growth in 1966–1967, if decline in population growth is taken into account. Two years' growth seems permanently lost for Egypt.

Second, and more important, the growth prospects are particularly bleak for Egypt because the increase in the level of defense expenditure, induced by the present state of affairs, largely has been "financed" by a fall in the share of gross capital formation to levels that cannot possibly sustain a growth rate of about 5.5 percent in the longer run. In addition, there has been a "capital-loss" through military actions (the destruction of the canal zone cities, in particular) that has to be made good.

The relevant data are set out in Table 2. Defense expenditure increased from 7.4 percent (average for 1960–1961 to 1964–1965) to 13.0 percent of the GNP in 1969–1970 while expenditure on gross capital formation fell from 18.2 to 13.0 percent for the same years. An investment ratio of 13 percent can hardly sustain more than 3–4 percent growth. The relatively high growth rate from 1968–1970 was partly due to recovery after the recession of 1966–1967 through increased capacity utilization, partly the result of accruing benefits from the Aswan High Dam, that is, from old investments. There may be some more benefits to follow from the High Dam but clearly Egypt cannot be expected to continue growing by 5.5 percent at her present level of investments. And without increased foreign aid, investments can hardly be increased at the present level of defense expenditures. A decline in the growth rate to about 4 percent is already now clearly discernible.

Israel's position in this regard is entirely different, and she does not directly seem to face serious difficulties with the growth rate, even at a continuation of

---

[3] Because of crop fluctuations it is appropriate to consider the average of 1968–1969 and 1969–1970 for Egypt.

Table 2

Defense Expenditure, Gross Investments, and Foreign Deficits Shares in GNP, Egypt and Israel
(Percentages)

	Egypt		Israel	
	1960–1961/1964–1965	1969–1970	1960–1965	1970
Defense expenditure	7.4	13.0	6.9	20.6
Cross capital formation	18.2	13.0	31.3	27.3
Foreign deficit, goods, and services	4.6	4.1	21.1	22.8

Note: National accounts data except defense expenditure, which is identified with budget expenditures officially classified under Defense. These may include some civilian expenditure and may not include all military expenditure. Other sources indicate even higher levels of defense expenditure in both countries.

Sources: Egypt–Central Department of Mobilization and Statistics, Cairo. Israel–*Statistical Abstract of Israel,* 1972, and earlier issues.

the present high level of defense expenditure. The very strong increase in defense expenditure from 6.9 to 20.6 percent of the GNP between 1960–1965 and 1970 has only been financed to less than one-third from a fall in the rate of gross investments,[4] that is, from 31.3 to 27.3 percent, and with only a minor increase in the foreign deficit; the main source of financing has been a fall in the share of private and public civilian consumption. Recalling, moreover, that annual population growth in Israel fell by about one percentage point from 1960–1965 to 1970, and taking the capital:GNP ratio to be somewhat above 3, it will be understood that investments in 1970 only slightly fell short of what was needed for sustaining about the same rate of growth per capita as during the period from 1960–1965. However, a large increase in the immigration to Israel could seriously magnify the problem.

Little information is available for the other Arab countries, including those directly involved in confrontation with Israel. Some of them publish only national income estimates at current prices; their estimates are not very up to date and they are highly uncertain.

The Lebanese economy had problems in connection with the Intra Bank crisis before the June war of 1967. As a consequence of this crisis and the war, tourism, trade, and construction experienced setbacks. In 1968 the growth rate was negative, but in 1971 and 1972—with the revival of tourism and an increase

[4] For comparisons in absolute terms it is useful to recall that, converted into U.S. dollars at official exchange rates, the GNP of Egypt in 1970 was only slightly higher than that of Israel—$6.5 billion against $5.4 billion. In 1973, the GNPs of the two countries must be approximately equal in size (calculated at unchanged exchange rates).

in the inflow of capital from some of the oil-producing countries—it may have reached growth rates of about 7–8 percent. Defense expenditures have increased, but are still very modest. The long-term growth rate, perhaps of the order of 5 percent, has probably not been affected by the war despite armed clashes between the Lebanese Army and Palestinian guerillas and the Israelis.

The Syrian economy was almost stagnant from 1965 to 1968, but that was more the result of poor crops than of the war. The years 1971–1972 saw a sharp upswing in the economy which was mainly the consequence of bumper crops. The general growth rate has been modest, about 5 percent per year between 1963–1965 and 1969–1971, and has been generated mainly in some of the service sectors such as transport and government. Agriculture was completely stagnant and, disregarding oil, industrial growth was only about 4 percent per year. It is difficult to pinpoint specific adverse consequences of the war, but it stands to reason that growth prospects must have suffered from the large defense expenditures. Although for Syria, the Israeli occupation of the Golan Heights was a minor problem from an economic point of view, their occupation of the West Bank was a blow to the roots of the Jordanian economy despite the resumed trade relations between the East and West banks.

Jordanian official estimates show an increase of the GNP at current prices by a total of 10 percent from 1967 to 1970. In real terms, the annual increases must have been negligible. The estimates are difficult to appraise because they somehow include the West Bank. However, separate national income data (official Israeli estimates, that is, and thus presumably not underestimations of progress) are available now for those Arab territories occupied by Israel. The relevant data are shown in Table 3. It is not clear from the sources of the data how Jewish colonies and military establishments in the occupied territories have been dealt with, that is, whether they are included in the Israeli or the occupied-territory GDP; therefore, it is not obvious how these figures should be interpreted.

At face value, the growth rates of domestic production (GDP) within the occupied territories are quite satisfactory. The high GDP rates of the West Bank in 1969–1970 can presumably be ascribed to recovery after the war and the first disorganization caused by the occupation, and thus may be considered as a temporary phenomenon. For 1971, the rate of GDP was 6.6 percent which seems to be below the average of about 8 percent experienced by Jordan between 1954–1955 and 1965–1966, although it seems to be considerably higher than the present growth rate for the East Bank. The rate of GDP for the Gaza Strip and Northern Sinai was somewhat higher: 7.9 percent in 1971, after a very high rate in 1970, which probably again can be ascribed to recovery. What the growth rates may have been for these territories before the war is not known.[5]

[5] Sinai was, of course, included in the Egyptian GDP, while the Gaza Strip, to the best of my knowledge, was included nowhere.

Table 3

GDP, GNP, and Growth Rates in the Occupied Territories
(Million Israeli Lire Unless Otherwise Stated
and at 1968 Constant Market Prices)

Territory	1968	1969	1970	1971
*West Bank**				
GDP	335	377	411	438
Factor payments from abroad	17	47	68	117
Less Factor payments to abroad	7	7	8	8
GNP	345	417	471	546
Growth rate of GDP (percent)	–	12.5	9.0	6.6
Growth rate of GNP (percent)	–	20.9	12.9	15.9
Gaza Strip and North Sinai				
GDP	130	138	165	178
Factor payments from abroad	2	8	21	30
Less Factor payments to abroad	3	3	3	3
GNP	129	143	184	207
Growth rate of GDP (percent)	–	6.2	19.6	7.9
Growth rate of GNP (percent)	–	10.9	28.7	12.5

*Judea and Samaria in Israeli terminology.
Source: Statistical Abstract of Israel (Jerusalem, 1972) Table XXVI/7, pp. 648–649.

On the other hand, the growth rates of national income (at market prices), or the GNP, are very high, ending with 15.9 percent for the West Bank and 12.5 for Gaza and Northern Sinai in 1971. The difference between GDP and GNP rates is due to the development of "factor payments from abroad," which mainly consists of wages earned by Palestinian workers employed in or by Israel, although substantial amounts are remittances from Palestinians working in Arab countries or overseas. It might be argued that the GDP rates look much more impressive when evaluated against the fact that a significant part of the labor force in the occupied territories is employed in or by Israel. However, unemployment was high before the occupation (refugees in camps, etc.), and to the extent that unemployed have taken work in Israel, the GDP of the occupied territories should not suffer because of increased employment in Israel. But it seems clear that agriculture has been drained for some of its labor force (partly attracted by the relatively high wages in Israel, partly because West Bank farmers are squeezed between high costs and low East Bank prices) and since the Arab West Bank farmers do not have the capital resources and the know-how needed for shifting to more capital-intensive cultivation there is a tendency for Arab land to go out of cultivation, and this by itself tends to reduce the GDP.

The income earned by Arabs working as Israeli employees adds, of course, to the per capita income and standard of living in the occupied territories and directly implies both growth and development. Such income tends to have multiplier effects on the GDP (services, etc.). However, were the occupation suddenly brought to an end, thus ending the Arabs' employment by or in Israel, it is doubtful whether the period of occupation would have added much to the growth potential of these areas. The Arabs are largely employed in lower-rated occupations with little new to learn; whereas the dissemination of technology is largely confined to the Jewish colonies.

In Iraq the Baath regime is pushing strongly for growth so that growth rates may be substantial. Iraq is not directly involved in the war and her financial position is very good. Being an oil producer on a large scale, she really belongs to the group of rich Arab countries (see below). It would seem that, despite the uncertain political situation (including the Kurdish problem), the government has started a number of ambiguous development projects which, if successful, may help to overcome the backwardness of the country.[6]

The Arab oil countries have seen spectacular increases in their foreign revenues and national incomes during the last few years. The rapid economic development of these countries is, in a sense, rather uninteresting because it is a simple consequence of the developments of the international oil market: If you have large oil deposits, you cannot help growing fast. If, in addition, as a producer, you stick together with other producers to increase oil prices and royalties, your income will grow very fast, so fast, indeed, that you will not know how to spend it.

For the area, considered as a whole, the extraordinary income growth and accumulations of financial capital of the oil countries have, however, important economic consequences to which we now turn.[7]

II. The Financial Position of the Middle East

It is not possible to set up a complete financial balance sheet for the Middle East showing total foreign debts and assets by countries. However, Tables 4 and 5 should indicate the general financial situation.

We have divided the Arab countries into two groups, the poor and the rich. The group of poor Arab countries includes those directly involved in the conflict with Israel together with the two Yemens, the Yemen Arab Republic (YAR) and the People's Democratic Republic of Yemen, (PDRY). The rich Arab countries include, in addition to the oil-producing ones, Lebanon, which benefits finan-

[6] *The Economist* (London) 248 (No. 6781, 11–17, August 1973) 32–33.
[7] The special problems about production, pricing, and taxation of oil are outside the scope of this discussion. [Author's Note (March 1974): The exorbitant price increases for crude oil at the end of 1973 and the beginning of 1974 exacerbated the problem of the huge liquid reserve accumulations of the Arab oil exporters. But the problem was already there before these price increases. What was a big problem has become a huge problem and from the point of view of development in the Middle East nothing was really changed qualitatively.]

Table 4

Surplus in Foreign Current Transactions: Goods and Services Plus Transfers
(in Millions of U.S. Dollars)

Country	1966	1967	1968	1969	1970	1971	1972
1. YAR	n.a.*	n.a.	n.a.	−16	−38	−19	n.a.
2. PDRY	n.a.	−11	−35	−5	−8	−12	n.a.
3. Egypt	−179	−286	−245	−296	−450	−475	−460
4. Syria	−51	−33	−30	−61	−73	−80	−16
5. Jordan	−92	−78	−120	−174	−128	−163	−194
6. *Total* poor Arab countries	(−322)	(−408)	(−430)	−552	−697	−749	n.a.
7. Transfers to government†	110	308	407	424	416	367	n.a.
8. Lebanon	−114	−42	−18	−20	−15	−17	n.a.
9. Iraq	17	65	185	181	100	192	n.a.
10. Saudi Arabia	86	83	−8	5	107	902	n.a.
11. Kuwait‡	566	460	510	543	651	1215	n.a.
12. Qatar	n.a.	n.a.	n.a.	50	45	66	n.a.
13. Bahrein	n.a.	n.a.	−11	−6	3	10	n.a.
14. Libya	7	121	335	446	848	909	n.a.
15. *Total,* rich Arab countries	(562)	(687)	(993)	1199	1739	3277	n.a.
16. *Total,* Arab countries	(240)	(279)	(563)	647	1042	2558	n.a.
17. Israel, goods and services	−440	−531	−718	−869	−1234	−1227	−1075
18. Private transfers§	286	532	441	465	666	771	996

*n.a. = not available.
†Not including the two Yemens.
‡Financial year 1 March–28 (29) February
§For Israel, donations from abroad appear statistically as private transfers; for the poor Arab countries, they appear as transfer to government.
Source: I.M.F., *International Financial Statistics* (several issues) items 77a and 77ta; information in the I.M.F.

cially through a substantial inflow of capital from the oil countries. Here "rich" means really "financially strong." In rich Arab countries with high per capita incomes, appalling poverty is nonetheless widespread, with Kuwait probably the only exception; and in rich Iraq, even per capita income is low. The poor Arab countries, on the other hand, are poor in every sense of the word: They are financially weak, their per capita income is low, the large majority of the population lives in poverty, and they are even poorly endowed with natural resources.

The poor Arab countries are running persistent, increasingly large balance-of-payments deficits. In 1968 the deficits were fully covered by grants from the rich Arabs, but from 1969 on the grants have not covered the deficits, and the poor Arabs are now again rapidly increasing their substantial foreign debts (see

Table 5

Net Foreign Assets: Banking System, End of Year
(in Millions of U.S. Dollars)

Country	1968	1971	1972
YAR	70	96	114*
PDRY	72	72	69
Egypt	−303	−615	−564
Syria	−49	−43	−36
Jordan	295	254	273
Total, poor Arab countries	85	−236	−144
Lebanon	532	1,022	1,328
Iraq	438	592	765
Saudi Arabia	889	1,776	3,174
Kuwait	1,806	2,451	3,912†
Qatar	113	192	264
Bahrein	83	125	137
Libya	532	2,684	2,951
Total, rich Arab countries	4,392	8,841	12,531
Total, Arab countries	4,487	8,605	12,387
Israel	628	477	n.a.

*September
†Including liquid reserves kept by Ministry of Finance

Table 4). Their total annual deficit (including payments for, and not deliveries of, military equipment), which before the June 1967 war amounted to about $300 million in U.S. dollars, had by 1971 risen to above $700 million. Even considering inflation and the devaluation of the U.S. dollar, a real increase of their deficit has occurred, both absolutely and in relation to real GNP.

Adding up the deficits of the poor Arab countries from 1966–1971 we reach the figure of $3 billion. Of this cumulative deficit, about $2 billion has been covered by grants from the rich oil countries; borrowing thus amounted to about $1 billion. Adding to that another $0.5 billion incurred during 1972–1973, and recalling that Egypt's total visible foreign debt in 1966 alone amounted to about $1.5 billion, it will be understood that these countries together may have a visible debt of some $3–4 billion at the end of 1973. To this amount, we should add unknown debts for delivery of military equipment (perhaps closer to $2 billion than to $1 billion), which yields a total debt of about $5 billion at the end of September 1973.

The rich Arabs, on the other hand, have experienced a spectacular increase in their total balance of payments and surplus from about $0.6 billion in 1966 to $3.3

billion in 1971; the surplus has most certainly been larger during 1972 and 1973. And note that of the smaller oil sheikdoms with rapidly growing incomes, Abu Dabi and Oman are not included. For 1973, the surplus of the rich Arab countries on foreign transactions in goods and services may have exceeded $4 billion. Cumulating the annual surplus over time and considering grants to other Arab countries, it would seem likely that the total net foreign assets of the rich Arab states will exceed $17 billion at the end of 1973. At the growth rate of some $4 billion per year, they would reach $40 billion by 1980. These are significant amounts, even in the context of international high finance.[8]

A very substantial part of the Arabs' foreign assets is kept in highly liquid form (see Table 5). Once more, we have to distinguish between poor and rich Arab states. While the five poor countries had net liquid liabilities of $0.1 billion at the end of 1972, the seven rich countries held net foreign liquid assets of $12.5 billion, increasing by about $4 billion per year. Thus, the net liquid assets of the Arab countries as a whole seem to have trebled over four years, from $4.4 billion at the end of 1968 to $12.5 billion at the end of 1972. At the end of 1973 the figure may have increased to about $16 billion.

Needless to say, the energy crisis and the oil shortage looming over the United States with the oil producers' price, royalty, and participation policies accelerate Arab financial capital accumulation and liquid reserves.

Two important observations follow directly from these facts: First, on balance, the Middle East is potentially more than self-sufficient with capital, even at very high rates of real domestic investments in the Arab deficit countries. In 1971, the deficits of Egypt, Syria, and Jordan would only absorb one-fifth of the rich Arab countries' combined surplus. In fact, at present the latter do finance a substantial part of the deficits of the former, through grants and loans. With high rates of investments in the three deficit countries (and correspondingly higher deficits), they would still absorb less than half the 1973 surplus of the rich. More than sufficient amounts would remain for financing even the large goods-and-services deficit of Israel!

At present, there is a certain flow of capital from the Communist countries to the Middle East (Egypt and Syria), a somewhat larger flow (including transfers) from the West (the United States) to Israel and Jordan, and a much larger flow from the rich Arab countries to the West. The capital inflows could be elim-

---

[8] Forty billion by 1980 is a mechanical extrapolation based on September 1973 prices and production and not really a forecast. A genuine forecast would have to consider separately the likely increase in oil revenues, which again depends upon production, prices, and producer shares, as well as growth of expenditures (including purchases of military equipment). My best guesstimate would be some $70–80 billion at the end of 1980 at September 1973 prices. But forecasts of $200 billion by 1980 have appeared in the press (*Neue Zürcher Zeitung,* 22 August 1973, p. 20). [Author's Note (March 1974): Such figures were grossly exaggerated at the prices ruling at that time, but after the last oil price hikes $200 billion is certainly on the low side. Annual accumulations of about $50 billion from 1974 have been predicted by the World Bank.]

inated through financing of the area's investments by the area's own savings, even at a substantial increase in the real investments of the deficit countries.

Second, the liquid reserves of the rich Arab countries are already now large enough for playing a significant role in the world monetary system. Should Arab reserves move away from the U.S. dollar (in which a substantial part of them seem to be or have been invested) into other currencies or into the free gold market, the dollar would go down the drain, unless European central banks were willing to support the dollar—which seems unlikely. There are other big investors in the gamble around the dollar but in a short time the rich Arabs will become the most influential ones, and even the whole U.S. gold reserve and drawing rights on the International Monetary Fund (IMF) would not suffice to fight off a speculative attack on the dollar from their side. Arab money is powerful, and might become hot, even militant. Used for financing development in the poor Arab countries, this capital would finance purchases of capital goods from the developed Western countries and, in this way, a substantial part of the money would flow to the United States considering the improving competitiveness of the United States. The United States has a very positive interest in getting the rich Arabs to invest their liquid capital on a long-term basis, and should, for purely egotistic reasons, be interested in creating conditions that would tempt the rich Arabs to invest for a long term. In fact, already in the summer of 1973 the U.S. government, at a meeting in Paris of the "group of twenty," expressed concern over the implications of the large liquid reserves of the Arab oil countries for the international monetary system, and suggested that part of their reserves be invested more permanently. (We shall return to these problems in the section entitled, "VII. Development Perspectives.")

One of the reasons why the oil countries keep such large liquid reserves is simply that it takes time to make good investments, and at the speed with which their assets grow, it is impossible for these countries to prevent their liquid reserves from growing. But part of the problem stems also from the difficulties encountered by the rich Arabs in finding what they consider safe investment outlets. Hence, the recent mocking suggestion of the Saudi Arabian Minister for Petroleum Mr. Yamani—to solve the balance-of-payments problem of the United States by direct investments in American business!

Our two observations naturally lead to the conclusion that safe, long-term investment outlets for the rich Arabs' reserves should be created in the Middle East itself. And since there are relatively few sensible investment outlets apart from petrochemical industries in the Arabian Peninsula itself, this would, for all purposes and intents, mean loans to the other Arab countries. The capital problem of the deficit countries in the area would thus be solved, and it would positively contribute to stabilize the world's foreign exchange markets in general, and the dollar and the free gold market in particular. A crucial problem here is: at what interest rates and other loan conditions the rich Arabs could and would lend to their poor brethren.*

III. Capital and Development

While the region as a whole is rich in financial capital and much more than self-sufficient, the fact remains that the area is divided into financial haves and have-nots. Since the June war of 1967 the Arab financial have-nots have relied heavily upon grants from Arab oil countries for covering their balance-of-payments deficits (Table 4, row 7), while Israel during all of her existence has relied even more upon donations from American and European Jewry (Table 4, row 18). Note that the grants to the poor Arabs are declining while those to Israel are rapidly increasing. The four belligerent countries have very high defense expenditures and are unable now to keep investments at desired levels although as mentioned earlier, much less so in Israel than in Egypt, Jordan, and Syria. Therefore, the question is, how important capital really is for development in these countries.

Israel is the only Middle Eastern country that has fairly reliable data bearing upon this problem. Even for this country there is considerable uncertainty about the contributions to GNP growth of the input of the basic factors, labor and capital, and of factor-productivity (the *residual*).[9] Even so, the picture is reasonably clear: Capital has been and probably will continue to be crucial for maintaining a high growth rate in Israel.

The main results of growth and productivity calculations for Israel are set out in Table 6. The following features are noteworthy: First, GNP growth in Israel has been highly and increasingly dependent upon capital. For the period of 1950–1955, the mechanical calculations behind Table 6 ascribe about 38 percent of the growth attained to increased capital input (Table 6, column 7 over column 8); for 1960–1965, the corresponding figure was about 51 percent. Developed countries are generally much less dependent upon capital in their growth process (according to this kind of calculation).

Second, productivity of capital has been falling during the whole period of 1950–1965, while productivity of labor has been increasing strongly. Falling productivity of capital is a rare phenomenon in developed countries. This fact reflects, of course, an exceptionally strong increase of capital per worker, but it may also be a sign of inefficiency in the use of capital.

*Author's Note (March 1974): After the latest oil price increases these problems extend to Europe, Japan and many less-developed countries. Here, however, we are only concerned with the specific Middle East problems.

[9] In statistical analyses of GNP-growth it is a standard method to divide the increase of GNP into two parts: one part which can be ascribed to an increase in the input of labor and capital at given productivity of these factors; and another part, called *the residual* because it comes out in the statistical analyses as the unexplained rest of the increase of GNP. It expresses increased average factor productivity, but the problem is then exactly why factor productivity has increased.

Table 6

Israel: Annual Growth Rates of Inputs, Product, and Productivity (Percents)

Years	Factor Inputs		Productivity			Weighted Input Contribution to Product Growth		Product (8) = (5)+(6)+(7)	Product per Man (9) = (8)−(1)
	Labor (1)	Capital (2)	Labor (3)	Capital (4)	Total ("the residual") (5)	Labor (6)	Capital (7)		
1950–1955	6.5	17.4	5.5	−4.3	2.8	4.9	4.7	12.4	5.9
1955–1960	4.0	11.2	5.3	−1.5	2.9	2.6	4.0	9.5	5.5
1960–1965	4.7	10.8	4.2	−1.5	1.8	2.7	4.6	9.1	4.4

Note that we have preferred to use calculations that include government and take into account the errors and omissions item in the balance of payments. The argument against including government in such calculations is that productivity in government is by definition constant. The inclusion thus pulls down all figures for productivity increase. However, government is a fact of life, and for comparisons with similar calculations for other countries it should be included. How to treat the errors and omissions item is a highly debatable matter. Its inclusion lowers the productivity increase for both labor and capital, and increases the relative importance of capital, but the overall picture remains the same.

Source: A.L. Gaathon, *Economic Productivity in Israel* (Jerusalem: Bank of Israel and Praeger, 1971), Table A–13, p. 205: 1.a, Total economy, adjusted.

Third, the *residual* factor, the increase of factor productivity (that is productivity of labor and capital together, considered as one factor of production), is not particularly high in Israel as compared with that of other developed countries. On an adjusted basis (see Table 6), the Israeli residual factor for 1950–1965 was lower than that of Japan, West Germany, Italy, Yugoslavia, the Netherlands, and France, and was equal to that of Sweden, but higher than that of Canada, Norway, Belgium, the United Kingdom, and the United States. [10] Moreover, it shows a clear downward trend, falling by about one-third from 1950–1955 to 1960–1965 (no matter which basis is used); according to the figures in Table 6, it has fallen from 2.8 to 1.8 percent. During the period of 1950–1955 about 23 percent of the increase of the GNP could be ascribed to the residual factor; for 1960–1965, the corresponding figure was about 20 percent.

Thus, contrary to widespread popular opinion, Israel does not seem to have benefitted much in its fast GNP growth upon whatever is behind the residual factor—for example, improved education, innovations, and so forth. It is the inflow of labor backed by massive capital investments that have achieved success and, to a large extent, the latter have been based upon a massive inflow of cheap capital (e.g., loans, grants, compensation payments, and, above all, donations) from, particularly, the United States. And the mediocre residual factor seems even to be declining in importance for whatever reason.

It is understandable, therefore, that Michael Bruno in his contribution to this project expressed some concern about future growth in Israel,[11] although certain factors such as the decreasing need for investments in infrastructure, large-scale irrigation, and housing, with the lower rate of increase of population, point to lower capital requirements in the future. The possibility of the need for large investments in water-desalination plants counts in the opposite direction, however, and the prospects of population growth are uncertain.

While it is difficult to conceive of anything that should lead to an increase of the residual factor in Israel (see below), to me it would seem that, whereas obviously capital investments have been the key to the rapid increase of labor productivity, concern about capital supply in Israel is largely unwarranted despite the heavy dependency upon foreign capital and donations. The reasons for this are listed below.

At a continued *status quo* post bellum, Israel can presumably rely upon continued support from the United States although the dollar devaluations could perhaps cause trouble: Given amounts of grants and donations in terms of

---

[10] A. L. Gaathon, *Economic Productivity in Israel* (Jerusalem: Bank of Israel and Praeger, 1971), pp. 78, N. 1 and 79; *The Residual Factor and Economic Growth* (Paris: OECD, 1964), p. 15. On the unadjusted basis, the Israeli residual factor for the total economy was higher than that of Yugoslavia and the Netherlands, and equal to that of France.

[11] Michael Bruno, "Economic Development of Egypt," in Cooper and Alexander, eds., *Economic Development,* pp. 93–157.

dollars have less real value in terms of non-American goods and services, and neither Congress nor donors may feel that they should increase their dollar contributions just because the dollar has been depreciated abroad. And it is crucial for Israel that the share of loans should not increase: Grants and donations carry no debt service charges.

At a complete, genuine termination of the hostilities, permitting a return to the prewar level of defense expenditure, the fall in defense expenditure would permit a simultaneous increase of the share of investments to the level of 1960–1965, alongside a very substantial improvement of the balance-of-payments deficit from 22.6 percent of GNP to "only" 13.1 percent—provided, of course, that the share of private and public civilian consumption remains at its present level. Although this share is by no means low as compared with other developed countries, the main risk for economic policy in Israel is that genuine peace in the Middle East might lead to domestic demands for a higher share of consumption (private and public civilian) and less willingness from foreign donors to cover the balance-of-payments deficit. Under such circumstances it might even be difficult to preserve the present share of gross investments unless there is increased reliance upon foreign loans; in any case, the growth rate might begin to be threatened, in particular if the country should have to rely on loans at market rates of interest rather than donations. Who can permanently borrow 20 percent of the GNP annually at interest rates of 10 percent or more?

The most unfavorable situation one could imagine for Israeli growth prospects is perhaps a situation of peace in which the United States and American Jewry feel that there are no longer security problems for Israel, so that they reduce donations with the Israeli government still wanting to keep the military machinery at its present level. Should immigration increase, in this situation, and the demands for increased consumption become irresistible, the growth prospects might become very bleak.

We have discussed the significance of capital investments for Israel in so much detail, not only because it is important for that country and the data are available, but also because, at a much lower level of growth rates for inputs, outputs, and factor productivity, and much smaller balance-of-payments deficits and donations, the problems of the poor Arabs in many ways resemble those of Israel.

Egypt has very incomplete data on overall capital and labor inputs, but existing information indicates that when development and the increase of per capita income reached a peak during the first half of the sixties, it was largely the result of a strong increase in capital investments, almost exclusively financed from abroad (by the United States and the USSR), while little can be ascribed to the residual factor, perhaps 0.5 percent.[12] Thus, Egypt's residual factor may

[12] Robert Mabro and Patrick O'Brien, "Structural Changes in the Egyptian Economy," in *Studies in the Economic History of the Middle East,* ed. M. A. Cook (London, 1970) pp. 412–427.

have been only one-fifth of that of Israel's and even less as compared with the fast-growing developed countries in the West and East. It follows that high growth rates of the GNP in Egypt (like those of so many other poor countries) will require exceptionally high rates of capital investment, higher than could conceivably be attained even under favorable conditions of financing, unless, of course, financing can be obtained from the wealthy Arabs or from the discovery of rich oil fields in Egypt, a possibility which still cannot be ruled out. On the other hand, a fall in the investment ratio is particularly damaging to per capita growth. With a residual factor of about the order of magnitude of population growth, per capita income will remain unchanged, even if gross investments fall to a level where only replacements of existing capital are made. Without a significant residual factor, per capita growth can easily become negative.

In conditions of genuine peace, Egypt should be able to switch the defense and investment shares of the GNP back to her 1960–1965 pattern. It is doubtful, however, whether that would suffice for a satisfactory growth performance in the future. Not only does Egypt have to catch up for the years lost in terms of both investments and growth rates; it also stands to reason that future capital requirements will be larger than in the past, measured per percentage unit of growth rate. Moreover, as in the case of Israel, the present sponsors in the Arab and, to a minor extent, the Communist worlds may not feel obliged to finance deficits through donations any longer, once genuine peace is established. For a country with the low per capita income and the relatively slow growth of Egypt, it may finally be more difficult to keep consumption down in the long term than it is in a high-income, fast-growing country like Israel, although that is perhaps not so obvious because differences in the political structure may become decisive factors.

Of the two other directly belligerent Arab countries, Jordan's situation is particularly difficult to appraise because of the Israeli occupation of the West Bank. Before the war of June 1967, Jordan relied heavily upon capital inflow from abroad (the deficit was 12–15 percent of the GNP). On the other hand, she seems to have attained a rather high growth rate at a low rate of investment (about equal to the inflow of capital) and to have enjoyed a residual factor of perhaps 2–3 percent.[13] Information is unreliable, however, and all of it may be a matter of statistical illusions. The share of investment in the GNP of Jordan seems to have fallen from about 15 percent in 1966 to 12 percent in 1970; the present GNP growth rate is probably less than 2–3 percent, and in the future Jordan will certainly be much more dependent upon capital investment than she was in the past.

Syria enjoyed an expansion of oil production during the sixties which tends to show up as a residual factor, vanishing again when the expansion of oil produc-

[13] Michael P. Mazur, "Economic Development of Jordan," in Cooper and Alexander, eds., *Economic Development,* p. 225.

tion slows down. In the long run this does not seem to be a growth factor that can be relied upon. The Euphrates Dam, financed by the USSR, should, however, give Syrian agriculture a boost during the next five years through a substantial expansion of the irrigated area. The investments needed for this purpose have largely been made, but, despite some important extensions of the transport network in recent years, Syria is still so much in need of infrastructure that its future development depends heavily on capital investments.

Lebanon benefits from a substantial inflow of capital from the rich Arabs and thus has no long-term capital problems, although it has felt the turbulence of the world's short-term capital movements during recent years. Iraq, finally, is the only one of the Arab oil countries with substantial domestic investment outlets. Belonging to the rich Arabs, the country has no capital problems except that of striking the right balance between domestic and foreign investments. But then, on the other hand, she has domestic problems (the Kurds) that might lead to higher military expenditure in the future.

IV. The Residual Factor

A high *residual* factor—that is, a rapid increase of factor productivity—is a boon for any country with GNP growth, total or per capita, on the program. It is in the interest of any such country to seek an increase in the residual factor, provided, of course, that the costs of education, acquisition of patents, know-how, etc. necessary for increasing the residual are smaller than the growth-equivalent investments in real capital.

During the sixties, high hopes were pinned to education as being the basic factor underlying the residual. These hopes appear today to have been exaggerated. It is becoming increasingly clear that education is far from the whole story. Israel, with her high standards of education and relatively low residual factor, is a case in point. Moreover, rather than contributing to GNP growth, present educational policies and practices in less developed countries seem, in fact, to contribute to the creation of a rapidly growing urban "proletariat" of unemployed graduates from secondary schools and universities, who are unable to find jobs that correspond to their education and, above all, their aspirations. Misdirected educational policies, emphasizing higher, liberal education in urban areas rather than professional education, vocational training, and primary education in rural areas can be blamed for a considerable part of the failure of educational efforts.

The Arab countries, particularly Egypt, are no exception in this regard. University and secondary school education has been expanding at tremendous speed, with the expansion concentrated upon the liberal arts, commerce, and law, with few employment possibilities except in government offices. There has also been a sharp deterioration of the quality of education as a consequence of the fast quantitative expansion, with teachers being drowned in students and examinations. Despite some limitations on admittance, even the old professional university departments in Cairo—engineering, medicine, and agronomy—which in the past have held very respectable standards in all their activities, now have experienced a serious decline in quality of education. Egypt has largely avoided the academic unemployment problem by extending to all graduates the right of employment. Practically, this policy has led to overstaffing in all government offices, public enterprises, and organizations. It could, ideally, have been used for forcing graduates into teaching and other governmental activities in rural areas, where there is often a serious shortage of educated manpower; but, more often than not, the graduate has a relative or acquaintance who can put him into an office in Cairo or Alexandria. On top of the decline in the quality of education, Egypt has experienced a serious drain of adequately (often foreign) educated professionals who, during the last decade, have left the country at an accelerated tempo. A substantial number have, however, been absorbed by the rich Arab countries and here they may contribute to development in the area.

Albeit on a much smaller scale, the situation is much the same in Jordan, including the Palestinians, and in Syria. Lebanon has pursued an old-fashioned policy with the emphasis on private education. In addition to being unsocial, the Lebanese educational system is also entirely inadequate from a developmental point of view.

To what extent education in the Arab countries can be slowly redirected toward a more productive pattern remains to be seen. The organizational problems are overwhelming, and the present cohorts of students have become an important political pressure group that may succeed in twisting the educational systems even more in the wrong direction. In any case, a restructuring of the educational system will take a long time, and it will take even longer for its effects on production to appear. The year 1980 will be unaffected by whatever reforms are initiated now; the year 2000 may see the first benefits of such reforms.

More hope can be attached to innovation in agriculture. Recent experience in Mexico, the Philippines, India, and Pakistan, and, among the Middle Eastern countries, Turkey has shown that the so-called green revolution may add substantially to growth in a relatively short period. Abstractly speaking, the green revolution amounts to embodied technical progress insofar as some capital investment is needed to make the innovation work. In both wheat and rice, the new high-yield varieties require fertilizers, pesticides, and water. In previously irrigated areas, the investments of capital required are small (although in poor, backward countries they are large enough to be a real obstacle), but if irrigation has to be arranged for, capital costs may be high or even prohibitive. The new high-yield varieties are, moreover, highly location-specific. Thus, the new Mexican wheat varieties give poor results under Egyptian soil and climatic conditions.

The green revolution does not come like manna from heaven. Nonetheless, there is undoubtedly much scope for agricultural improvements in the area.

There is no reason to expect that Israel should be able to increase her residual factor through green revolution. Israeli agriculture is already highly advanced and has pioneered in the introduction of both new varieties and methods of cultivation. It is unlikely that the process of agricultural improvement within Israel could be speeded up further. In addition, it should be recalled that in Israel agriculture is rapidly diminishing in importance, and that the growing water shortage might have adverse consequences for her agricultural productivity. A spillover of technology into the occupied areas is likely to occur, but with the present Israeli land and settlement policies in these areas, it is doubtful who will benefit. Otherwise, it is clearly the Arab countries that stand to gain from the green revolution.

In a sense, green revolution is nothing new for Egypt. When long-staple cotton was introduced and developed during the nineteenth century, that was, of course, nothing but green revolution in the modern sense of the phrase. The systematic development of new cotton varieties in the 1920s and 1930s by British cotton experts working in Egypt is another case in point. The strong increase of the rice yield in the early forties and of corn in the early sixties are other such instances.

Despite the long historical experience of Egypt with improved plant varieties, the new Egyptian regime concentrated its efforts during the fifties and until the late sixties mostly on so-called horizontal expansion of agriculture, being more fascinated by spectacular reclamation projects such as that of the Tahrir Province, than by *vertical* expansion concentrating on increasing yields and improving crop composition on the existing cultivated area.

The Aswan Dam should imply a substantial contribution to vertical development in that it should lead to a strong increase of rice growing (a relatively profitable crop), a shift from low-yield autumn (flood) corn to high-yield summer corn, and the conversion of large, one-crop areas into double or treble cropping. Expectations have been fulfilled insofar as rice and corn are concerned, but, strangely enough, the total crop area has not expanded much more than the total cultivated area, a fact which points to reclamation rather than to conversion of one-crop into two-crop areas.

More generally, efforts in Egypt have not been sufficiently concentrated on the development of new plant varieties and on increased input of chemicals. In wheat, one of the largest crops by acreage, selections from ancient *baladi* varieties dominated until a few years ago, when finally a new high-yield variety was developed locally. Until recently it was primarily the cash crops (above all, cotton) that attracted the attention of the Egyptian (government) plant scientists. Inputs of chemicals have increased strongly, but they are still way below the optimum. Israeli destruction of Egyptian fertilizer plants has hampered the expansion of fertilizer production, but the suboptimal fertilizer consumption is largely the outcome of misdirected governmental investment policies.[14]

Also, crop composition has not really attracted the attention of the authorities. During the sixties, cropping patterns were clearly suboptimal due to governmental intervention with both prices and acreages for field crops.[15] The cultivation of fruit and vegetables has increased substantially over the last two decades, largely as a response to domestic, urban demand. For export purposes, the introduction of new varieties and standards is badly needed. With the present institutional setting this must be a governmental problem, but little seems to have been done in this direction. For one of the traditional export crops, onions, it would even seem that quality has deteriorated the last few years in connection with overwatering. It may be worth noting that, whereas at the present level of technology there are probably no large-scale advantages in the agricultural production process itself (apart from irrigation and, perhaps, soil preparation, which the cooperative system ideally should take care of), fruit and vegetables grown on a commercial, export scale may enjoy economies of scale in production. If that is so, it has consequences, not only for the land-reform plans of the government (aiming at further diminishing the maximum holding to 25 acres), but also for the government's present emphasis on improving cultivation methods on the small production units (of 3–5 acres). If the government wants to promote production of fruits and vegetables for export, it may have to permit large private farms.

Syria has a different problem than Egypt's. While, in Egypt the importance of crop rotation is well understood by the peasants, and fallow land is the exception, Syrian farmers still have to learn the benefits of rational crop rotation and break away from the ancient fallow-land cultivation methods that prevail, even on irrigated lands. Rotations with pulses and feed-crops seem highly promising for radically increasing the agricultural output, not only on irrigated land, but also where dry farming is practiced. On irrigated areas, the introduction of new high-yield varieties promises an additional increase in output. Mexican wheat varieties thrive in Syria and the acreage planted with these high-yield varieties was expected to reach 12 percent of the total wheat area in 1972. Progress seems to be slow, however. These changes in cultivation methods would greatly benefit animal husbandry, through providing feed on a large scale. Many of the same considerations hold true for Iraq.

Despite much more intensive land cultivation in Lebanon and Jordan, these countries also stand to gain from more rational rotation methods. In Lebanon,

[14] Bent Hansen and Karim Nashashibi, *Foreign Exchange Regimes and Development, Egypt: From Manchester Liberalism to Arab Socialism* (New York: N.B.E.R. and Columbia University Press, forthcoming), chap. 9.

[15] *Ibid.*, chap. 7; and Wyn F. Owen, "Land and Water Use in the Egyptian High Dam Era," *Land Economics* Vol. 40 (No. 3, August 1964) pp. 277–293.

some obviously profitable large-scale irrigation projects along the Litani River have gone unrealized for years because of political obstacles. According to official (rather unreliable) estimates, the GDP in agriculture at current prices fell slightly in the years 1966–1971. Other estimates show some increase, but it is abundantly clear that governmental efforts to improve Lebanese agriculture are entirely inadequate.

In each of these four Arab countries, increased progress through the residual factor would require various institutional changes. In all countries, rapid progress in agriculture requires governmental action. Egypt has the machinery to implement such change, but at the top there seems to be a lack of understanding of the problems involved. In the other four countries—particularly in Lebanon and Syria—the machinery itself is missing or, at least, is too rudimentary. Traditionally, some of these countries have had little government (except colonial government, of course), and Lebanon is still characterized by a noninterventionist attitude that hampers all concerted effort for bringing about change.

In relation to industry and trade, it is Egypt that stands to gain in terms of the residual. The country has adopted Arab socialism, which, for all intents and purposes, means public ownership of big business in all walks of life and the nationalization of foreign trade and payments. Without implying a centralized command-economy, the system has, as a matter of fact, implied substantial interference with both prices and production, and transferred all major investment decisions to the government.

Studies of industrial investment planning in Egypt during the fifties and sixties have revealed some glaring cases of large-scale investments that should not have been made, not just with the wisdom of hindsight, but also from what could reasonably have been foretold.[16] Iron and steel (based on Aswan ore) and automobile assembling are two such examples. While big money was wasted in these industries, other industries suffered from lack of funds for modernization (e.g., the textile industry) or expansion (e.g., cement). In some industries the choice of technique has been inoptimal. There are instances where it seems that such mistakes could not possibly have been made by private, profit-oriented decision makers. In any case, Egypt stands to gain much from improved investment planning.

Israel, in fact, has had in the past—and to some extent still has—the same kind of problems with industry as does Egypt, and for similar reasons. With her exchange controls, multiple exchange rates, and other kinds of interference with the price system, along with a large public or semipublic sector, Israeli industry has suffered from inefficiencies related to unfortunate investment decisions and doubtful choices of technology.[17] During recent years, the country has moved

[16] Hansen and Nashashibi, *Foreign Exchange,* chaps. 8–10.
[17] Michael Michaeli, *Foreign Exchange Regimes and Development, Israel,* (N.B.E.R. and Columbia University Press, forthcoming).

in the direction of private entrepreneurship and free trade, but it remains to be seen whether this change in the system really has implied an increase of the growth rate.

V. The Institutional Setup

These brief remarks on inefficiency in production through government intervention of various kinds lead to the more general question of the role of institutions for economic development, particularly whether the institutional setup in the Middle Eastern countries is conducive to development or if the opposite is true. Interpreting the notion of *institutions* in a broad sense to include the socio-political system there is little doubt that the institutions of the Arab countries are a serious obstacle to their growth, so serious, indeed, that it is questionable whether rapid sustained growth can be expected unless profound institutional changes take place.

Generally, an immense expansion of the bureaucracy has been the most conspicuous feature of Arab socialism in Egypt. With bureaucracy, has come inefficiency in investment, production, and trade decisions; here is a point where change could only be to the better.

However, to change the system is not a simple matter. In the first place, there is the necessity of finding forms of organization and decision making that would work better under conditions of *government ownership* of big business and foreign trade. Indeed, we meet here a problem facing all socialist systems. The Communist countries have not succeeded in solving the efficiency problem, and perhaps it may be asking too much to require Egypt to solve it. But then, of course, a country should not adopt a system that it does not know how to handle. I do not believe that the problems of public ownership to the means of production are so intractable as the failures of the Communist countries might indicate. Ideological prejudice has hamstrung their efforts of finding solutions to their problems. Since, however, the Arab countries—Egypt, at least—are not hampered by orthodox Marxist ideology and prejudices, they might have better possibilities for moving toward more efficient forms than have the Communist countries. The exchange reforms recently undertaken by the Egyptian government may be taken as a step in this direction, although it does not really change the basic features of the system and may only be a return to the multiple-rate systems of the fifties. There are other signs indicating that Egypt is turning her back to socialism, but governmental ownership and control of the economy remain a basic fact of her economy.

The greatest obstacle to reform in Egypt is that, with the passage of time, vested interests in the conservation of the system have grown up and become strong. And when the groups that have vested interests in the existing system also constitute the ruling class, fundamental changes may be well-nigh impossible to achieve. This is precisely the situation in Egypt. Being essentially a dictatorship based on the power of the army, a layer of people in influential and remunerative positions (civilian as well as military) has slowly been formed, upon which the power of the president ultimately depends, who, in their turn, depend entirely upon the benevolence of the president and his cabinet. This is the ruling class and the economic "aristocracy" of the country; they have an interest in conserving the system, and they wield the power to do just that. The *Times* of London has characterized the present governing class in Egypt as bourgeois—and the *Times* should know. However, the bourgeoisie has always fulfilled a productive function (nobody understood that better than Marx), and its income and power has always been related to its wealth. The Egyptian ruling class today does not consist of really wealthy people. In this regard, its members are at the most middle class. More often than not, they have no productive functions, and they derive their incomes from what they can extract from the establishment. They are essentially a parasitic class, fulfilling no other function than that of conserving their own positions and preventing the system from being changed.

The revolution of 1952 and the nationalizations of 1961–1963 deprived the old land-owning and industrial bourgeoisie of their power base and established a system that undoubtedly was intended to be more egalitarian and socially more advanced than was the old system. But at the top, the old bourgeoisie was replaced by the upper layers of the army and bureaucracy, and whoever happened to be or to become favored by the rulers. Since the old traditions of nepotism were not eradicated, but mushroomed as never before, the upper bureaucracy proper and enterprise management (after the nationalizations) were slowly surrounded by armies of so-called assistants, advisers, experts, consultants, specialists, and whatnot, all having no function other than that of obtaining a good income. This parasitic class has to be weeded out as one of the preconditions for increased efficiency and growth in Egypt.

To change the system in this regard would require not only a major political effort, but also a profound change in attitudes of people in general. Nepotism is not something that has been imposed upon the country against the will of the people. It is a way of life that has to be changed. The shift to a well-balanced market economy would not by itself change these attitudes, but there is little doubt that it has flourished so wildly during the last decade because of the increasing imbalances in the economy and the government's attempts to solve the problems administratively. If prices and exchange rate, together with budgetary policies, could be adjusted so as to create balance between demand and supply everywhere in the economy, including foreign trade; if management of nationalized enterprises in production, as well as in trade, could be ordered to maximize profits and be authorized to act accordingly, and be paid in proportion to profits—then nepotism would have much more limited possibilities for making itself felt. It should be noted also that incentive pay to management (and workers) does not necessarily require large absolute differences in income. It is worth noticing that the big government-owned hotels (the tourist industry) to some extent are run by private management, and seem to work efficiently.

Little information is available about the efficiency of the few industries in Syria and Iraq. Both countries have adapted the Ba'ath brand of Arab socialism, and investment decisions are firmly in the hands of government. Both countries have experienced a strong increase in the bureaucracy and in this regard, as in most others, they resemble Egyptian Arab socialism. So far, however, Arab socialism may have been less damaging to economic growth of Syria and Iraq than to that of Egypt. It can probably be argued that at present it is even improving the immediate growth perspectives in Syria and Iraq. Their growth processes, both in agriculture and industry, are still in their infancy. Decisions to be taken are rather obvious and simple (e.g., dams, canals, cement plants, fertilizer production based on gas, to mention a few examples). At this stage of development, governments may achieve better results than would private entrepreneurship. It is when the economies become more complex and sophisticated that governments begin to face serious difficulties in running the economy and become inferior to private enterprise. All this is well-known from communist countries.

The problem is not only one of growing economic complexities, however. There is, in addition, the problem that *stability* in totalitarian systems (and without stability they do not reach the state of complexity) is conducive to the emergence of a parasitic class without genuine development interests surrounding the rulers. It would probably be wrong to claim that Syria and Iraq have already reached this state. Erratic and unpredictable though they are, and torn by internal strife, the small Ba'ath parties have been devoted to both development and socialism in a way that the present ruling class in Egypt has never been. Syria and Iraq have not yet suffocated under the bureaucracies they are hatching. But the writing on the wall is clear. The Syrian regime has, during the last few years, liberalized conditions somewhat for the remaining private businesses and the effect appears to have been beneficial for the economy. However, as in Egypt, their real problem is the large public sector, including all the nationalized businesses, and in this regard there seems to have been no important changes in the institutional machinery.

If, on the other hand, the Ba'ath regimes should prove *unstable* in the longer run, as they have certainly been in the short run, we encounter development problems of another type, only too well known to Arab countries. Political instability is everywhere detrimental to economic growth, and the Arab world is no exception. We emphasize this well-known fact because a prolongation of the *status quo* post bellum may induce political upheavals in the Arab world, while a resolution of the conflict that can be considered just from the Arab point of view probably will be conducive to political stability.

Lebanon has very different institutional problems. Her liberal attitudes toward private business make the country something of a haven for private entrepreneurship and its growth rate seems to have been significant. Private entrepreneurship is neither a necessary nor a sufficient condition for growth, however. Moreover, the uneasy political balance, together with widespread corruption in government, parliament, and administration block all necessary reform to overcome backwardness in the countryside. The still-unsolved Litani River irrigation problem is the outstanding example, but the problem is the same in education, health, and other fields.[18]

VI. East and West Trade

Like other developing countries, those of the Middle East have difficulties with their exports to the developed countries where trade restrictions often block the road for those commodities (e.g., agricultural products and textiles) that the developing countries can deliver. To some extent, the complaints of the developing countries are exaggerated. Thus, Egypt, like India, does not even use up her export quotas to the United States and Europe according to the long-term textiles agreement arranged by the General Agreement on Tariffs and Trade (GATT). The explanation is partly lack of competitiveness, which could be rectified through adequate exchange-rate policies, and partly lack of capacity, which could have been expanded through more adequate investment policies. Nonetheless, the trade obstacles are very real, and an expansion of exports to the Western world would be conducive to development through the increased supply of convertible foreign exchange. Some of the Arab countries— for example, Egypt, Syria, and Iraq—have clearly overdeveloped their trade with Communist countries and would benefit from a certain shift toward the West.

It is important in this context that recent developments in the policy of the EEC point to entirely new perspectives for the trade of the Mediterranean Middle East. I refer to the decision in 1972 by the EEC Council to open negotiations about favored treatment to all Mediterranean countries. What may come out of this decision is difficult to say at present. It has been met with stiff opposition from the United States on the basis that it limits the scope of free international trade. Initial negotiations between the EEC and Spain and Israel do not seem to have led very far, the conditions of the EEC being considered unattractive by these two countries. The EEC is reluctant to give concessions in regard to agricultural products, including fruits and vegetables, and their derivatives, apart from off-season trade with fresh products; and in regard to industrial products, reciprocity is a major obstacle.

Leaving the general problem of the EEC and the freedom of world trade, there is little doubt that the Middle Eastern countries could benefit greatly from some

[18] Adel Kanaan, "The Political Economy of Development Planning: The Case of Lebanon," (Ph.D. diss. University of California, Berkeley, 1972).

kind of association with the Common Market, and they should probably not be reluctant to accept reciprocity if that could lead to significant concessions for exports of agricultural products (raw and processed) to Europe.

Considering the present strong tendency for agricultural terms of trade to improve vis-à-vis industry, less developed countries have good reasons for playing down their industrialization efforts somewhat in favor of increased emphasis on agriculture. It is to be hoped that the same trend may help to soften the Continental European (especially the French) attitudes to agricultural protection.

The Mediterranean Middle Eastern countries could have a splendid future as the vegetable and fruit garden of Europe, being placed in much the same geographic and climatic position as California and Florida in the United States. Canning and processing of vegetables and fruit would then be a natural proposition for industrial development. Egypt, Lebanon, and Jordan would be the main beneficiaries, but Israel, too, would clearly gain from the abolition of agricultural protection in Europe. If only off-season exports were permitted this would still greatly benefit Egypt which is able to grow most vegetables all the year round.

VII. Development Perspectives

In the previous sections, a number of circumstances have been discussed that in various ways give rise to a reappraisal of the economic development possibilities in the Middle East. Considering the slow progress in the search for a peace formula that is acceptable to the adversaries, or one which the Great Powers are prepared to impose upon both sides of the conflict, the point has been reached where the developmental prospects of individual countries should be considered against the background of alternative outcomes of the conflict in regard to future frontiers, rather than be evaluated on the basis of complacent developmental assumptions for each country considered in isolation. The two alternatives which most naturally come to mind—without implying anything about the actual outcome of the conflict—are those of peace based upon the U.N. resolutions recommending a territorial return to the *status quo* ante (1967) bellum with minor, economically insignificant frontier adjustments, and a continuation of the *status quo* post bellum with *de facto* annexation of the occupied territories. We shall disregard the possibility of new military operations with the territorial consequences they might imply. And we shall also leave aside the possibility that Israel, with continued occupation and annexation, might expel the Arab population to give room to a large inflow of Jewish immigrants.

The territorial issues are themselves of minor consequence for the developmental prospects of the area as a whole or even for the development of individual countries, with Jordan and the presently occupied territories themselves being the obvious exceptions. The assumptions chosen in this regard do, however, have a direct effect upon several factors of general importance for development in the area, such as levels of defense expenditure, political stability, and patterns of trade in the area. More indirectly, the outcome of the conflict may affect capital supply (including donations and grants) to the area and EEC policies and general world trade conditions. Thus, we have also to make assumptions about the latter two factors. Needless to say, the assumptions could be blended in other ways than those we shall consider, and an infinity of alternatives could be presented.

We shall consider three alternatives only, two extremes and an intermediary possibility. With *status quo* ante bellum in regard to territory, we can imagine a state of genuine peace with the lion(s) and the lamb(s) grazing peacefully together and cooperating in all possible ways. This alternative may look like a rather utopian dream. Nonetheless, we shall concentrate the discussion on this *Alternative 1* because it brings out all the potentialities of the area and, clearly, it is the best possible economic alternative for both Arabs and Jews. As an *Alternative 2* we shall retain the assumption of *status quo* ante bellum in regard to territory, but disregard the possibility of economic cooperation between the Arab countries and Israel. From an economic point of view, this alternative is inferior to Alternative 1 for everybody involved. Alternative 2 falls clearly between the extremes of Alternative 1 and our *Alternative 3* which assumes territorial *status quo* post bellum without, of course, any kind of cooperation between the Arab countries and Israel. This alternative is economically the worst one for everybody, including Israel.

Alternative 1: *Status Quo* Ante Bellum with Full Economic Cooperation

This alternative implies the most optimistic development projections, not only for the Arab countries, but also, as we shall argue, for Israel. It is the only alternative which gives promises of a genuine peace that would permit full disarmament of the area with defense expenditures being reduced to normal or even to a token size everywhere. Moreover, it is the only alternative which offers promises of political stability for the Arab side. This may mean a strengthening of essentially inefficient regimes so that political stability could lead to the conservation of economic inefficiency. However, we optimistically shall assume that the stabilization and strengthening of the present regimes would induce them to undertake the institutional reforms so badly needed, particularly in Egypt. There is nothing in the logic of the situation which says that would necessarily happen, but then it is difficult to visualize any other situation that by necessity would imply more efficient Arab regimes.

Finally, it would seem that it is the only alternative which offers conditions under which the Arab side overtly could accept adopting normal trade and other economic relations with Israel. Since some trade is always better than no trade—so we are taught by well-established economic theory—developmental prospects for both Arabs and Israel should benefit from the opening of trade.

It has been argued that the opening of trade would essentially be to the benefit of Israel, and that it might even be harmful to the Arab countries. The argument is partly based upon the conception that Israeli industries should be more advanced and efficient compared with Arab industries so that the latter would have no chance of competing on equal terms. Moreover, it is argued that Israel might become an inroad for American capital to the poor Arab countries. In both ways, a foreign hegemony over the Arab economies might then be established. Quite apart from nationalistic and ideological considerations, such arguments have been an important aspect of Arab fears about the consequences of opening economic relations with Israel.

It would appear today that these fears are largely unfounded.[19] First, as we have already noted, Israeli industries are generally not very efficient in their use of resources. In the past they have depended greatly upon almost unlimited supplies of cheap or even cost-free capital and, in addition, are now troubled by strong cost-inflationary tendencies from the labor side. Some of their apparent successes in exports to developed countries have partly been conditioned by the support of Jewish communities in such countries. Economically, Israel does not generally stand out as a fierce competitor. Recent studies show that, even at the current official exchange rates, some of the better Egyptian industries would have no problems in competing with corresponding Israeli industries.[20] It should be recalled also, that competitiveness is conditioned by the choice of exchange rates and if, after the opening of trade, the poor Arabs should turn out to run large deficits, the solution would be to devalue their currencies (granted, of course, that their fiscal and monetary policies were adequate), which already now they are in need of.

Second, Israel does not have a surplus of capital, and with the emergence of the huge funds of the rich Arab oil countries it is doubtful how competitive in capital the Americans really will be in the future. In addition, there is nothing in the opening of trade with Israel which compels the Arabs to dismantle existing controls with inflows of foreign capital and the establishment of foreign-owned enterprises.

Nonetheless, it is probably true that Israel would stand to gain more from the opening of trade than would the Arabs. Economically, the Arab world, with all the developing countries that for ideological reasons have little or no trade with

[19] In my earlier contribution to this study, I was somewhat in doubt about the justification of these fears; see Hansen, "Economic Development of Egypt," in Cooper and Alexander, eds., *Economic Development*, p. 85.

[20] Bent Hansen and Karim Nashashibi, "Protection and Competitiveness in Egyptian Agriculture and Industry," Working Paper, (Washington, D.C.: National Bureau of Economic Research, to be published).

Israel at present, is much larger than Israel. Thus, it would be Israel, more than the Arab nations, who would benefit from expansion of the potential trading area.

More important, however, is the fact that the Arab countries—more concretely Egypt and Lebanon, and perhaps also Syria—are able to supply Israel with a commodity which the latter cannot import from other countries (except at prohibitive transport costs). Earlier we mentioned Israel's water supply problem. A point seems to have been reached where the opportunity costs of water for Israel are the costs of desalinating sea water. At known technologies these costs are very high. Unless they can be lowered, Israeli agriculture and other heavily water-consuming industries may be in jeopardy. At present cropping patterns Egypt has surplus water; substantial quantities of water pass unused into the Mediterranean Sea. So far, Lebanon has not made use of the water of the Litani River. The piping of water from the eastern branch of the Nile (about 200 miles along the seashore) and from the Litani might be cheaper than desalination of sea water; yet, piping the water to Israel might afford Egypt and Lebanon a higher income than the potential returns obtained from their own domestic utilization of the water. If so, Egypt and, to a much smaller extent, Lebanon would have a source of foreign revenue as good as oil (even better because it would never dry up); and Israel would have a cheaper solution to her water problem. Syria has surplus water, too, in the Euphrates, but the piping distance is longer (about 300 miles) and the terrain more difficult. A project like this one presumes, of course, a very high degree of confidence between the countries involved and looks entirely utopian against the background of present realities; but here we are only speaking about a possible state of genuine peace and its economic potentialities.

To the assumptions of low or even negligible defense expenditures, stable efficient governments, and the opening of trade between Israel and the Arabs, let us add the establishment of arrangements for investments of the rich Arabs' capital in the area[21] and favorable trade conditions in the European Common Market. As a consequence, the stage obviously has been set for relatively fast growth in all countries of the Middle East, at least in the longer run. In the short run the poor Arab countries, notably Egypt and Jordan, would continue for some time to suffer from the effects of destruction and low levels of investment since 1967 (for Egypt, since 1965). For both of these countries, as well as for Israel, there would be some adjustment problems to overcome when territories are handed back to their owners. Thus, for instance, West Bank and Gaza Arabs would

[21] The Kuwait Fund for Arab Economic Development was established about ten years ago with a capital of $350 million. An Arab Fund for Economic and Social Development is under formation, but without Saudi Arabian participation; its capital is yet undetermined. The money involved here is peanuts, however, compared with the liquid capital now under accumulation.

suffer a substantial setback in income unless Israel continued to keep her labor market open for foreigners; under conditions of genuine peace there is no reason, however, why she should not prefer to do so. If, under present conditions, it pays for Israel to employ Arabs it will continue to be profitable, even though the West Bank and the Gaza Strip have to be given up by Israel.

The original projections made in this study used 1980 and 2000 as points of reference: It seems clear that, even under the present very favorable assumptions, Egypt would not be able by 1980 to reach the levels of per capita income projected earlier. The country now is lagging behind so far that there is no possibility of catching up by 1980. Jordan is a more difficult case, her future depending greatly upon that of the West Bank. With continued employment possibilities in Israel, the West Bank may attain a relatively high growth rate, no matter what its constitution and future will be. Incorporated by, or in federation with Jordan, it might keep the growth rate of Jordan high. A Jordan without the West Bank would have poor developmental prospects; this would be the case if the West Bank were established as an independent state, perhaps in federation with Lebanon. On the other hand, Lebanon, Syria, and Iraq, by present assumptions, should do better by 1980 than was earlier projected. And the same holds true for Israel, with one qualification: her future capital costs which have been discussed previously.

For the year 2000, all the Middle Eastern countries should show higher per capita incomes than those originally projected.

It is an intriguing problem to what extent the rich oil countries' capital could and would be used for the financing of such developments. Much would depend upon the terms of such loans; upon alternative possibilities of obtaining loans, grants, and donations; the possibilities of preventing domestic consumption from increasing too fast; and the extent to which countries like Egypt, Jordan, and Syria would be in need of consolidating their existing debts.

The rate of return actually obtained by the rich Arabs during recent years is not known, but most probably it has not been impressive. Their losses from dollar investments have been large, and substantial amounts have been given as subsidies to belligerent Arab countries (see Table 4); under conditions of peace (with the Suez Canal reopened)[22] such subsidies would presumably be abrogated. If, moreover, guarantees for debt service payments could be obtained from a Great Powers consortium, or from international organizations, so that all risks of default were removed, the rich Arabs might be willing to settle at relatively low interest rates.

---

[22] For a study of the prospects of the Suez Canal, in particular the possibility of increasing the capacity of the canal to accommodate supertankers, see Bent Hansen and Khairi Tourk, "An Economic Appraisal of the Suez Canal Project to Accommodate Super-Tankers," *Journal of Transport Economics and Policy* (forthcoming). A widening of the canal is, of course, an alternative to the pipeline project now underway. Incredible though it may sound, it appears that Egypt is planning to go along with both of these projects, each of which makes the other one superfluous.

Once peace is established, it seems clear that the oil-rich countries cannot be expected to invest really large amounts in the other Arab countries without guarantees for prompt debt service payments. Egypt, for instance, has a very bad record in this regard. Hence, the proposal for a Great Powers consortium to guarantee such payments. It might be asked why the Great Powers, particularly the United States and the USSR, should be willing to take on such an obligation.

First, considering the fact that much of the area's suffering is the result of power policies from the time of the British-French *divide et impera* policy after World War I to the present situation, it would be natural if the Great Powers now contributed positively to the establishment of genuine peace. The consortium could be part of the horse-trading leading up to the peace agreement.

Second, at a debt consolidation, with oil money used for paying the old external debts of the area, creditors would obtain convertible currency in return for more or less uncertain (nonconvertible) claims on the poor Arab states. The USSR, badly in need of convertible foreign exchange, would benefit greatly from this kind of arrangement.

Third, if oil money were used for financing future development, liquid reserves would be spent on capital goods and other goods, mainly in the Western world. Considering the improved competitiveness of the U.S. dollar, it stands to reason that part of these purchases would be directed toward U.S. products, thus improving the U.S. balance of payments and diminishing the world's short-term dollar claims. As mentioned previously, the United States is clearly interested in supporting this kind of arrangement; in fact, so are all other Western countries.

Fourth, it should be recalled that the risks that the consortium would undertake would be limited from the viewpoint of the consortium. The point is that the consortium members, adequately chosen, also are important trade-partners of the poor Arab countries. Should a country be in default, it would, at the next major bilateral trade negotiation, be confronted with its sins and be forced to refund (by running a bilateral surplus) to the Great Powers the amounts which they had had to cover.

Even at favorable interest rates, Middle Eastern countries would have no motive for borrowing from the rich Arabs so long as donations and grants can be obtained free of charge (and free from political strings). Here the mood of the developed world (including, in the case of Israel, that of the American Jewry) becomes decisive. The world may feel less inclined to give grants and donations, once genuine peace is established, but may, of course, also have agreed to increase such aid as part of the agreements leading up to a peace settlement. The general tendency is, however, for the developed countries to shift away from grants toward loans at market conditions, and in the longer run this trend would also apply to the Middle Eastern countries. Finally, the possibilities of domestic financing should presumably increase in the poor Arab countries, insofar as stable, strong governments should have a greater possibility of holding back domestic consumption. The very same circumstances might, however, lead to such high levels of investment that the result would be an increased need for foreign loans, even given the fall in defense expenditures.

It has already been indicated that the Arab Middle East deficit countries can only absorb a minor part of the rich Arabs' financial resources. These amounted already at the end of 1973 to a total of some $17 billion, with liquid reserves amounting to much the same amount. The total external debt of the poor Arabs was some $3–4 billion plus unknown military debts. Some of these debts have been obtained on favorable conditions (e.g., PL 480 counterpart funds) and may have no political strings attached to them (or the strings may have broken—e.g., PL 480 counterpart funds in countries that have severed diplomatic relations with the United States). Thus, only 20–25 percent of the rich Arabs' present liquid capital could conceivably be absorbed by (nonmilitary) debt consolidation. Adding debts for delivery of military equipment of, say $1–2 billion, the absorption of the presently existing total financial capital would still amount to less than one-third. And, even if conditions in the Middle East should become so paradisiacal that Israel could line up in the queue with her substantial debts (about $4 billion), only about half the rich Arabs' present liquid capital could be absorbed.

The rich Arabs' funds were in 1973 increasing at a rate of at least $4 billion per year. The poor Arabs' total deficit amounted to $0.7 billion 1971 (the last year for which data are available), and would thus absorb less than 20 percent of the present increase of the rich Arabs' funds. Even assuming that the total deficit would increase after the reduction of defense expenditures and the increase in investments, it is inconceivable that more than one-third could be absorbed. Israel's deficit under these conditions might amount to another $0.7 billion and could not bring the absorption above half the present increase of the rich Arabs' funds. Also, do not forget that the accumulation of the rich Arab countries is rapidly increasing.

Thus, we find that under no circumstances could more than half of the rich Arabs' present resources and accumulations be absorbed in the area. And as development progresses in the area, countries will probably prefer to shift from foreign to domestic financing and may even prefer to repay their debts. Investment in the Middle East is therefore, not only an insufficient, but also a temporary outlet for the oil-rich countries' financial capital; after a certain point, repayments may even aggravate the problem.*

Alternative 2: *Status Quo* Ante Bellum Without Economic Cooperation

We shall assume here that there is no economic cooperation between Israel and the Arabs, but that conditions are sufficiently peaceful to make all countries feel

---

*Author's Note (March 1974): After the increases of oil prices, the rich Arabs' funds are increasing, not by $4 billion, but rather by $50 billion per year. The other Middle Eastern countries can thus absorb only a trifle of the funds to be accumulated in the future.

that they could reduce their defense expenditures. (It might be objected that exactly under these conditions Israel would never reduce her defense expenditure; the reader can easily work out the consequences for himself: the more defense expenditure, the less development.) It follows from our discussion of Alternative 2 what the disadvantages would be and who would suffer from them.

All the countries would suffer from the ruined opportunities of trade expansion. Israel would probably suffer most, but the poor Arab nations and Lebanon could also suffer the significant[23] losses. If employment opportunities for Arabs in Israel were also cut off, the West Bank and Gaza would suffer a serious setback, which probably would not be compensated for through increased trade and employment opportunities in the Arab world. The West Bank and Gaza Arabs could, of course, easily be compensated through grants from the rich Arabs, but that would only relegate the problem to somebody else. Needless to say, developmental prospects by 1980 and 2000 would be less promising than under Alternative 1, particularly for Israel and Jordan (including the freed territories).

Alternative 3: *Status Quo* **Post Bellum**

Here we cannot assume that there would be economic cooperation between the Arabs and Israel; such cooperation, under these circumstances, would not be agreed to by the Arabs in any foreseeable future. Moreover, reduced defense expenditures seem excluded on both sides, while new arms races are a possibility that cannot be excluded. If the military machines are based on foreign equipment, the present balance-of-payments strain will continue for both Arabs and Israel, and may even be aggravated. If, on the other hand, sophisticated weapons industries are developed, like those which now exist in Israel and which Egypt is planning to set up, the social costs of defense will increase even more, and the balance-of-payments relief may be negligible. On both sides, the scale of production in such industries is so small that costs of production must become very high. All talk about spin-offs, externalities, etc. cannot hide this basic fact.[24]

From the point of view of the Arab countries, political instability may become the most serious consequence of continued occupation and creeping annexation. Whatever the political change, it would hardly be conducive to efficiency and growth. The domestic economies would not be kept in order, investments would not be promoted although financial aid would be available from the rich Arabs,

---

[23] In Hansen, "Economic Development of Egypt," p. 85, it was maintained that: "The Arab countries have lost little, in any case, in not having economic relations with Israel." This statement may perhaps be true for the past; for the future, the potential gains are probably significant.

[24] A very unpleasant possibility is that such industries might be developed into export industries, supplying governments in underdeveloped countries with weapons that, under present political constellations, cannot be obtained from either West or East. That might make such industries economical for the country itself, but would certainly not contribute to the welfare of the underdeveloped world.

and the regimes might not be able to, might not even wish to, benefit from better trade conditions in the EEC.

Under these assumptions little economic growth could be expected in Egypt and Jordan (East Bank), and even a decline in per capita income should not be ruled out.

For the occupied territories, per capita income and growth rates would remain higher than under Alternative 2, but not necessarily higher than under Alternative 1. With the territories under continued occupation, with Arab land tending to go out of cultivation, and with accelerated Jewish colonization, the Arab population would presumably face a future of being competed out from its own land (quite apart from the more direct methods applied by the Israeli Army), and of being employed as second-class labor doing the menial jobs for its rich master. They would, to be sure, achieve a higher, rapidly increasing material standard of living, but would be deprived of that dignity of man that is the ultimate aim of all development efforts.

For Syria, continued high defense expenditures would certainly slow down the developmental process; for both Syria and Lebanon, political instability might become the major threat to development.

Finally, it cannot be sufficiently emphasized that Israel also stands to lose economically under this third alternative. The occupied territories are poorly endowed with natural resources which can be exploited by Israel. Land is the only exception (apart from some limited deposits of oil and minerals in the Sinai) and for Israel (or rather her Jewish population) to benefit from the land, the Arabs will first have to be squeezed out; and heavy capital investments will be necessary. Considering the danger of threatening water shortages, it is doubtful how much social net benefit the Jews themselves would enjoy from their colonization of the West Bank and the Gaza Strip. The most important benefit for Israel is undoubtedly the access to unskilled Arab laborers. Even when these are paid Israeli union wages, the profits accrue to the Jewish employers. It is difficult to quantify the gain to Israel. In 1971, the occupied territories had factor payments from abroad amounting to 147 million Israeli Lire at 1968 prices. Part of these were remittances from emigrated Palestinians. Considering price increases and other circumstances, wages paid to laborers from the occupied territories may perhaps be about 200–250 million Israeli Lire in 1973. With a marginal share of labor in national income of about two-thirds, Israeli profits from Arab labor would amount to some 100–125 million Israeli Lire which again amounts to about 0.5 percent of the Israeli GNP. If the Arab laborers ease important bottlenecks in the Israeli economy, this figure may, of course, underrate the Israeli profits. Even adding possible profits from Jewish agricultural colonies, and some income from Sinai oil, it is clear that the Israeli economic gains from the occupation are trifling compared with the military expenditure involved in keeping the territories occupied (15–20 percent of GNP, say). Economically, the occupation is simply lunacy. But then, of course, it is not economic considerations that explain Israel's interest in annexing the occupied territories.

VIII. Concluding Remarks

Developmental prospects in the Middle East are at present entirely dominated by two major factors: the Arab-Israeli conflict and the huge accumulations of financial reserves in the rich Arab oil countries. It is the poor Arab countries that suffer from the conflict, and a continuation of the present state of affairs can only serve to widen the gap between the rich (Israel and the oil countries) and the poor, with a tremendous waste of resources for everybody involved. Our emphasis here has been upon the *economic* benefits to everyone from the establishment of genuine peace in the Middle East. And while the United States and the rich Arab nations certainly can finance an indefinitely prolonged *status quo* post bellum with ever-increasing defense expenditures, their money could instead become a great lever for future economic development.

Thus, economic development in the Middle East has become, to an unusual degree, a matter of political development. Politics will decide the outcome of the conflict between the Arab states and Israel; it will determine the willingness of the rich oil countries to invest their resources in the area; it will determine the domestic institutional conditions for economic progress in the poor Arab countries; and, finally, it will become decisive for the trade relations between the Mediterranean Middle East and the EEC. To project economic growth under these circumstances is a matter of conjecture, with economic rationality reduced to a secondary, or even more inferior, role.

PART II

The Political Outlook in the Local Arena

Malcolm Kerr

PART II

The Political Outlook in the Local Arena

Malcolm Kerr

As a chapter in an "overview" volume on Middle Eastern economic and political problems, presumably the discussion which follows should somehow represent a definitive distillation of available information and wisdom, much as years ago the evil chef sought to boil down Li'l Abner's pig to one magnificent drop of "ecstasy sauce." Unfortunately, that has not been possible. In what follows, interpretations are offered on rather arbitrarily selected aspects of three levels of political interaction within the Middle East: domestic Arab society, inter-Arab relations, and the conflict between the Arabs and Israel.

I. The Failure of Nasserism as a Belief System

With the Arab defeat in 1967 and, three years later, the death of the dominant figure of Arab politics in modern times, an era passed away which we may now begin to assess, tentatively and peripherally at least. Whether Nasserism is a term that will continue to have any currency now that Gamal Abdel Nasser is no longer there, and if so, whether it will have any generally agreed meaning, it is too early to tell; but it does seem clear that during his career he symbolized a range of attitudes and actions reaching far beyond Egypt and beyond the particular things he himself said and did. This being so, it might be expected that Nasserism, whether called by that name or not, should continue as a mainstream force in Arab politics, just as Kemalism continues to be very much alive (albeit in some difficulty) in Turkey. There are, after all, a whole series of regimes, parties, and movements in the Arab world, which generally look upon themselves as revolutionary, Pan-Arab, partially Marxist but non-Communist socialists, that grew up in Nasser's shadow and were nourished by his example. Even though some of them, like the Ba'athists in Syria, were bitter rivals of Nasser and his local followers at times and claimed to be critics of some of his policies, they are still part of the Nasserist phenomenon.

The writing of Part II was completed in December 1973.

This writer believes that Nasserism will have a rather different place in history than Kemalism, and that the general movement called by that name has entered a stage of decisive deterioration. It did not die with the June 1967 war, nor with Nasser himself, and some of its manifestations may be with us for many years, but the vitality, relevance, and credibility have gone out of it—and had already begun to do so, even prior to 1967. There are many dimensions to this proposition; in what follows we shall concentrate on the ideological character of the Nasserist movement, which perhaps may serve as a vantage point for assessing its other aspects.

At its broadest and most significant level, Nasserism is a movement of social and political reform whose highly nationalistic and activist spirit and pragmatic approach to policy decisions tends to conceal an eclectic, yet very conventional, neo-Islamic intellectual attitude. It is an overwhelmingly consensual movement, basically quite moderate by contemporary Arab standards; but the consensus and the moderation are the counterparts of an intellectual ambivalence that has marked the response of the educated classes of several whole generations of Arabs to the problems of adjusting traditional Muslim culture to the demands of modern secular life.

What used to be paraded by Arab intellectuals as simultaneously a revolutionary approach to life and a formula of happy compromise between indigenous traditions and imported technology has come increasingly to appear to them instead as an empty middle. This is especially the case since the shock of the Six-Day War, which seemed to reveal a previously unsuspected hard core of inadequacy in the whole Nasserist system and movement. It has now become quite fashionable in some Arab circles to criticize the Nasser legacy in severe tones for its "middlism" (wasatiya), to cite the expression of one of the currently best-known angry young men or Arab letters, Dr. Sadek Jalal al-'Azm.[1] The middle of what? Several things; the word implies a tendency to fall between two stools, both in terms of intellectual foundations and practical political decisions. The conventional Nasserite does not really know, and does not even know that he does not know, whether his outlook is secular or religious, democratic or authoritarian, universalistic or particularist, welfare-and-consumption oriented or saving-and-investment oriented; and he resorts, subconsciously, to shaky mental convolutions to paper over these wide-open ambiguities, so that the Nasserist nationalist-socialist-reformist-revolutionary-positive neutralist message can continue to be all things to all men, or at least to all Arabs. This is the criticism from today's outspoken group of critics, ranging from the Islamic fundamentalists such as Dr. Salah ad-Din al-Munajjid[2] on the right to 'Azm and other Marxists on the left.

[1] Sadek Jalal al-'Azm, *An-Naqd adh-dhati ba'd al-hazima (Self-Criticism After the Defeat)* (Beirut: Dar at-Tali'a, 1969), p. 134 ff.

[2] Salah ad-Din al-Munajjid, *A'midat an-Nakba (Pillars of the Disaster)* (Beirut: Dar al-Kitab al-Jadid, 1967); and *At-Tadlil al-Ishtiraki (The Socialist Misguidance)* (Beirut: Dar al-Kitab al-Jadid, 1965).

To grasp the roots of the Nasserist middlism and its failure, it is worth noting its background as an amalgam of the Islamic reformism and Arab nationalism of one and two generations ago. For the Arab socialists of today are entangled in much the same net of doctrinal inhibitions and equivocations as were the reformist religious thinkers of the past. The history of modern Muslim thought is replete with half-concealed efforts to hitch the transcendental appeal of religion to a succession of fashionable causes—scientism, constitutionalism, nationalism, and most recently, socialism. The most devout among educated Muslims have often tended to remain somewhat aloof from these efforts; for whether the purpose of the effort was to refurbish an image of religious backwardness, or to use religion as a commercial endorsement of political causes, it has been suspect in their eyes. For obverse reasons, the most committed secularists and socialists have also looked askance at the enterprise.

The mainstream advocates of Arab socialism do not, of course, lay claim to any special Islamic dispensation. They are content to assert that Arab socialism is consonant with the general principles of welfare, justice, equality, and brother-hood implicit in the Koran. They do not call for an Islamic state, or the enforcement of Islamic law; indeed, they regard the advocacy of such things as retrograde. Outwardly, therefore, it appears unjustified to place their thought in an Islamic context. The fact is, however, that they are very much concerned with elaborating a belief system of social morality for a society in which religious loyalty remains strong, a system attuned to the general moral culture rather than hostile to it. As nationalists, they do not believe that the ills of Arab society are due to anything fundamental in the Arabs' own traditions and values, but to various irrelevant distortions and accretions and external impositions—an attitude whose substance, if not terminology, has been inherited directly from the religious reformers.

The overtly secular ideas of Arab socialism possess an Islamic dimension just as the Islamic modernist-reformist movement possessed a political dimension. Psy-chologically and ideologically, if not logically or philosophically, the socialists represent a kind of extension of the age of both liberal and fundamentalist religious reformism, the first of these currents having led in Egypt a generation ago to the moderately secular constitutional liberalism of such figures as Taha Hussein and Ahmad Lutfi al-Sayyid, and the latter to Hassan al-Banna and the Muslim Brethren. It makes no logically consistent sense to reflect both of these opposing currents simultaneously, but the paradox dissolves as soon as we view the ideas involved not as intellectual propositions but as ideological ones, as expressions of the groupings of a harrassed and confused society for a set of convictions on which to base a sense of political and social direction.

Islamic reformism from the early nineteenth century onward was essentially a reaction to Western technological superiority. The stimulus was external, not internal: Muslims reexamined their beliefs not because of any crisis of con-science within their own society as in the European Reformation, but out of the necessity of self-preservation against the incursions of an alien culture. The external pressures have continued down to the present, and whatever problems Muslims now feel impelled to raise for themselves, whether in the religious or political realm, are unavoidable when projected against the background of an outside stimulus.

What mattered most in the ensuing dialogue but remained unsettled was whether modern Muslim society should derive its cultural, social, and political principles from external, that is, Western, sources. But the issue was only superficially geographical; more importantly, it was whether modernity must be post-Islamic. If it were, the implication would be that Koranic and other traditional teachings in many matters, especially in domains of public concern, were not "adaptable" so much as they were irrelevant. This dangerous and painful, if very real, issue was carefully sidestepped in most public discussions.

As an ideological movement concerned with the weakness of Muslim society in the face of foreign power, modern Islamic reformism has been as much a political as a religious phenomenon. Conversely, the dominant, explicitly political movements of the twentieth century in the Arab world—nationalism and socialism, eventually personified by Nasser—have not been altogether secular phenomena, even when their appeals and discussions leave religious terminology behind. Rather, there has been a transposition of religious symbols into secular ones, concealing an underlying continuity of psychological concerns and cultural issues. Just as an earlier generation of Islamic modernists sought to provide acceptance for elements of technological culture within an adjusted framework of Islamic appeals, so at a later time nationalists and socialists have sought to create institutions providing for the dignity, power, and progress of society within a framework of appeals to Arabism.

Beneath the surface it becomes very difficult indeed to distinguish the emotional force of Arabism from that of Islam; and the current debate between particularists and universalists within the nationalist and socialist movements of the Arab world today is essentially a counterpart of the past tensions between liberalization and fundamentalism within the Islamic reformist movement. What has changed is the terminology.

Between Islam and socialism, the connecting link is nationalism. It is through the medium of nationalism that the force of Islamic sentiment contributes a powerful impetus for the revolutionary activism and totalitarian vision that has characterized the most prominent embodiments of Arab socialism in recent years. Here we have a point of convergence—by no means accidental—between such mutually antagonistic movements as the fundamentalist Muslim Brethren and the progressive Nasserists and Ba'athists.

On the other hand, there are other important ways in which religion has constituted a restraint on the capacity of revolutionary movements in the Arab world to fulfill their apparent totalitarian potential. Here again we are concerned with symbols, but in a different way. Just as there are symbols of power and righteousness which are transposed from religious into secular terms, so also there are countervailing symbols of respectability and moderation which are transposed: For example, piety and propriety become, in secular terms, an attachment to law, order, and status. Furthermore, as political action proceeds, even those transposed symbols, which are initially supportive in nature, tend to break down at a certain point, raising new and painful realizations that the relevance of the indigenous cultural heritage (whether Islamic or Arab) has indeed come into question and can no longer be explained away by ideological obfuscation.

Arab socialism has risen to the fore as a particular expression of nationalism; and the debt it owes to Islamic sentiment is really part of the same debt owed by nationalism. It is true, of course, that on the face of it Arab nationalism is a secular force, but whatever nominal validity the secularist claims of nationalism may have on the level of formal ideas, they reflect no more than a tenuous psychological commitment among the masses. Arab nationalism has established itself as a vital force, not by offering a secular antidote to sentiments of religious solidarity, but, on the contrary, by avoiding any direct confrontation with religion.

The Arabs occupy a special historical position in Islam, and there is no inclination among nationalists to forget this. Their historical mythology and self-imagery is inextricably bound up with early Islamic history. The overlap in identity is symbolized today in the word *umma,* which may either refer to the (Islamic) "community" or the (Arab) "nation"; and the difference has remained no more than subconscious in a good many minds. Traditional Muslim sentiments have cherished the unity, dignity, and historic destiny of the *umma;* it is a simple matter today for the direction of these sentiments to be transposed from the community to the nation, without a break in continuity and without any occasion for agonizing reappraisals.

Eventually, conflicts of principle may arise, not over the question of identity, but over concrete social and political programs and actions. Once nationalists come to power they must identify themselves with some pattern of political organization and of socioeconomic policy. Two generations ago the *dernier cri* was constitutional liberalism; today it is revolutionary socialism. The fact that both these ideological models have originated as foreign importations has made it especially important for their Arab exponents to be able to justify them in indigenous, that is, Islamic, terms, showing that they are permissible or even positively endorsed by Islamic principles.

It has never been difficult to justify the simple notion of this or that fashionable ideological cause. Advocates of constitutional liberalism could point to classic Islamic precedents that appeared to sanctify progressive legislation, accountability of the ruler, toleration of competing viewpoints in a free society, etc. Similarly, socialists can invoke the Islamic virtue of almsgiving, the prohibition of usury, the primacy of public over private interest, and, above all, the ideals of brotherhood and equality among Muslims of high and low station. However contrived some of the interpretations of the Islamic tradition, the fact remains that apologetics along these lines have been widely successful in persuading many Muslims that no basic clash of modern and traditional (or imported and indigenous) principles was involved. The visible moral requirements of both *ummas* were satisfied, at least so long as it was possible to sidestep the question of where the inspiration for a given set of modern political ideas was really coming from. So long as only general ideas were at stake, this question could be glossed over easily enough. However, positive implementation proved more difficult.

The ideas of liberalism probably never penetrated except to the minds of a small, socially and intellectually privileged elite, who had been exposed to modern education. These ideas held some attraction for a time because they were associated with the material power of Britain and France. But when embodied in the constitutions of Egypt, Syria, and Iraq, they failed to produce any of the desired results, or even to function at all in the hands of their advocates on some occasions; and when constitutional regimes yielded to military dictatorships, little of real value seemed to have been lost. One obvious cause of the failure was the complete inability of the ruling classes of landowners and urban notables to respond to the social and economic needs of the mass of the population, and hence the inadequacy of a system of overt political values that emphasized formal procedures rather than the substance of public policy. Thus, the fact that a number of reasonably competitive elections were held now and then meant little, while the failure of elected parliaments to enact social reforms, especially agrarian reforms, meant everything.

A more subtle but equally significant cause of the liberal failure was the unresponsiveness of Arab and Muslim cultures to the kinds of political virtues that liberalism preached: particularly, the virtues of competitive and dynamic equilibrium among social groups and of the moral self-sufficiency of the individual; or more generally, the whole idea of organized action for public welfare being initiated from outside the confines of public authority. The dominant mentality among nationalists was one with deep Islamic roots, attaching central importance to collective virtues of society as a whole which could be achieved only through the state: power, prestige, solidarity, dignity, and rectitude. These virtues acquired a kind of urgency, moreover, in consequence of the vulnerability of the Near East to Western material superiority. If constitutional liberalism had a fault worse than the failure of its proponents to feed the hungry and clothe the naked, it was its inherent inability to provide a collective moral cause. It is hard for large numbers of people to get excited about ministerial accountability, because it does not evoke consciousness of familiar and significant values.

On this level of symbolism, the image of revolutionary socialism of the Nasserist sort offers a sharp contrast to liberalism and strikes directly at some inherited psychological needs as well as modern material ones. In so doing, it gives natural expression to both religious and nationalist convictions. It offers visions of advancement in the collective prosperity of the community, of harmonious rather than competitive relationships among individuals and groups in society, of equality and fraternity, of the furtherance of public morality, and of collective self-interest. These are symbolic values that respond simultaneously to the populism of the modern Arab nationalist and to the desire of the believing Muslim for a Straight Path to follow amidst the uncertainties of modern life.

What is especially important, in distinguishing these virtues from those of liberalism, is the mode by which they are provided: not by the uncontrollable, unfathomable interplay of disparate and unseen forces, but visibly and deliberately, by the concerted actions of strong leaders who truly embody the collective moral authority and destiny of the *umma*. Leadership is effectively confirmed not by an arbitrary and stylized process of competitive election, in which conflicts of ambition and interest are legitimized, but by a combination of popular acclamation and adherence to the path of righteousness. The acclamation with which a man like Nasser was received by the masses was a manifestation of the revolutionary socialist component of this formula, while his struggle against the forces of darkness—imperialism and social oppression—reflected the religious component. But these two elements are not mutually exclusive, for Islamic sentiment is also populist, and socialist sentiment is also righteous. Socialists and believers alike can approvingly recognize a political ethos in which the *umma,* through its leader, forcefully asserts its collective will for the sake of a just cause; they also can welcome the spirit of devotion to common duty and of striving for the Right that is the essence of *jihad.*

However much the Arab socialist movement may have been indebted to religious and nationalist sentiment for its moral stimulus, it was not such sentiment that inspired the ideas of socialism in the Arab world in the first place. The main doctrines themselves were imported from Europe by Egyptian, Syrian, Iraqi, and Lebanese intellectuals educated in British and French universities. The problems they detected in Arab society were by no means peculiar to the Arabs, and indigenous beliefs inherited from Islam offered no particular formula or strategy for attacking these problems.

The indigenous culture could hardly provide a diagnosis of its own society's ills, when in large part it had been the exposure to foreign culture that had revealed the existence of such ills in the first place. Nor could the indigenous culture define the concrete objectives of socialist reforms, or set practical priorities. All it could do was to provide a kind of topographical map for planners to take into account, showing some courses of action to be easier and more popular than others. This hardly amounted to providing socialism with its operational ideological foundations. Yet to acknowledge openly that the ideological foundations were not indigenous would be to stir up a hornet's nest, so strong is the continuing assumption that the Islamic message is one by which God provides a comprehensive and eternally relevant guide to life—or the nationalist message that Arab tradition does so.

All this has made for a curious situation. No exogenous doctrinal system addressing itself to the crucial social problems of the day can find wide and explicit acceptance, because the Islamic heritage, with its claim to universality— transposed in many minds to the "Arab heritage," but without quite relinquishing the universalist pretensions—preempts the field and blots out competing ideas from other quarters. Yet as we have noted, neither Islamic nor Arab social norms constitute an adequate basis for a clear and stable set of public goals and priorities, anymore than they did in the nineteenth century; and today, as before, Arab ideologists have fallen back on the practice of back-door borrowing of foreign ideas, and adapting their expression insofar as possible to the local culture in order to legitimize them as local products. Thus, today socialism is "Arab" just as at the turn of the century constitutionalism was "Islamic." Yet the ongoing process of implementing economic and social programs and making the necessary political choices seems to have been bound from the start to erode the self-assurance of those who preach the "Arab" character of the movement; and even before the crisis of 1967 brought this and other problems into such sharp relief, a *sotto voce* debate over the questions of universality had begun.

The most notable source of universal socialist ideas in recent years, of course, has been Communism, which not only claims worldwide applicability and a scientific basis, but has achieved impressive results in Russia, China, etc. In Nasserism, Ba'athist, and other mainstream Arab nationalist circles since 1960 or so, Marxist—Leninist concepts of exploitation, class struggle, imperialism, revolutionary leadership and organization, etc. gained considerable currency, so much so that the debate over universality does not call into question the general validity of these ideas but only the degree of their importance in relation to local nationalism and traditions and the extent to which they should be strictly and precisely interpreted. The debate is, in effect, a replay of the nineteenth-century polemics over the secular or Islamic character of liberalism, except that today, perhaps, more is at stake, since revolutionary socialism is so much more attuned to both the material problems and some of the cultural predispositions of Arab Muslim society and, therefore, carries a greater prospect for effecting major social changes—provided its thrust is not blunted by a creeping process of immobilization and adaptation to conventional middle-class Arab ways, as happened in the case of the liberal movement to a large extent.

This is what the Arab Marxist Left has feared—that parochial, respectable, middle-of-the-road, muddle-headed, well-meaning, reformist Arab nationalism, which lives on slogans and images, will smother the revolutionary message in an orgy of assimilation. Under Nasser, who was above all a nationalist and whose own intellectual convictions seem to have been fairly conventional however revolutionary his personal temperament, such a process was more or less in effect; under the God-fearing Anwar al-Sadat, even more so: Arab socialism is projected as being both scientific and culturally distinct at the same time. The unspoken, no doubt largely unconscious assumption is that this dual virtue arises from the Islamic basis of Arab culture: a transcendental and universalist faith, in which the Arabs have a special historic role. God will provide; nowadays what He provides is science, whereas a few decades ago He provided constitutions. But then He cannot very well be dead; and until He is, neither Marx nor Lenin nor Mao can come to life to point the way to a real overhaul of the society.

This may seem a captious thing to say. So long as the explicit religious formulas of society and politics are being abandoned, or at least transposed into secular formulas, does that not suggest a trend of modernization in the political culture? Not necessarily. Underneath the verbal formulas, the loyalties and values of a past age seem to be very much alive, continuing to limit the capacity of contemporary Arab society for the kinds of political and cultural innovations that a growing number of thoughtful people believe to be essential.

Although the weight of the Islamic heritage has its revolutionary as well as its conservative implications, it raises strong presumptions against the legitimacy of a political and moral order whose inspiration clearly comes from outside the confines of Muslim society. In today's parlance, this attitude takes the overt form of insisting that the principles of revolutionary socialism must be derived from distinctive Arab circumstances and experience. It is doubtful, however, that these really point in any particular direction.

However plausibly Arab socialist leaders may emphasize the compatibility of their reforms with religious prescriptions, the net impact of religion is obviously a conservative one which counteracts the mixture of scientism, experimentalism, Marxism, and sheer restlessness from which the revolution has gained much of its impetus thus far. Precedent has always been accorded great weight in the shaping of the moral prescriptions by which Muslim society has governed itself; and this imposes on innovators a heavy burden of presumption against the legitimacy of their actions and proposals. Like some of their counterparts elsewhere, Arab revolutionaries are in need of breaking through the barriers of conventionalism; yet, in order to win public acceptance, they are driven to cultivate an image of respectability.

The Marxist critique of Nasserism and other systems of Arab socialism has been expressed on many levels ever since the 1950s, but in Egypt itself only in a muted and tangential manner through such media as *at-Tali'a* magazine which the regime has tolerated as an outlet for its own tame ex-Communist intellectuals. Other Egyptian Marxists have done their publishing abroad in foreign languages.[3] Expression has been much freer in Beirut, where a small but solidly established Communist movement has published its own newspapers for many years and other leftist groups as well have openly debated the ideological questions of the day. But only since the June war have the shortcomings of the Arab socialist regimes and their followers been really loudly and systematically attacked from the Left; and nowhere has this attack been more vivid and provocative than in the pages of Sadek al-'Azm's book referred to earlier. For example:

Among the consequences of this lack of ideological clarity dominating the Arab socialist movement and predisposing it toward middlism is the futile argument over whether the socialism that the Arab revolutionary forces are supposedly calling for is "Arab socialism" or "an Arab application of socialism," and over whether our socialism is scientific or religiously faithful, imported or righteously guided, wise or Muslim, and so forth. The results of this confused thinking and verbal sophistry are reflected at once on the level of theory and practice. This future argument has no connection with any serious or important attempt to define the character of the Arab Left. In reality it does not go beyond feeble efforts to take advantage of the positive connotations the word "socialism" has acquired among the Arab masses, so as to justify positions and measures and policies that have nothing to do with scientific socialism. The articles written about verbal distinctions between "Arab socialism" and "an Arab application of socialism" are mere games to divert ourselves from the main subject that ought to command our intellectual and scientific concern, namely, scientific socialism itself. . . .[4]

As a result of this vagueness surrounding the ideas of the Arab revolution and the significance of its practical achievements, we are tyrannized by superficial concepts of what it means to base a socialist state upon the idea of the Arab revolutionary movement. I refer to concepts that do not go beyond the level of agrarian reform and nationalization (i.e., industrial reform), and attempts to create an atmosphere of improvement for the laboring classes by giving ownership of pieces of land to some of them or distributing shares of the profits of the factories which they have become the owners of by virtue of their being part of the public sector. These and other such measures emanate from a mentality that contributes to rotate in the orbit of an unstable and fluctuating concept of private ownership and does not yet embrace the scientific socialist concept of ownership.[5]

[3] See, for example, Anouar Abdel-Malek, *Egypte société militaire* (Paris: Le Seuil, 1962); Hassan Riad (pseudonym of Samir Amin), *L'Egypte Nassérienne* (Paris: Editions Minuit, 1964); and Mahmoud Hussein, *La Lutte de classes en Egypte de 1945 à 1968* (Paris: Maspéro, 1969).
[4] al-'Azm, *Self-Criticism*, pp. 135–136.
[5] *Ibid.*, p. 138.

Al−'Azm goes on to attack Nasserism on other fronts as well, and calls attention to "the negative form in which Arab political slogans cast their causes, such as 'the non-capitalist road,' 'positive neutralism,' 'non-alignment,' and 'the Third World,' which is supposed to be half way between the first and the second world; . . . 'non-exploitative ownership,' 'dissolution of the differences between classes,' and 'the non-dominance of one class over another.' "[6]

Perhaps these intellectual weaknesses, which after all are easy enough for critics to point out, are of little practical consequence. For one thing, the middlist spirit of compromise and consensus seems to reflect a very real need for social harmony amidst the pains of social modernization and political vulnerability in the world. Would the Arabs really be better off fighting each other over ideological fine points? An obvious retort to this is that they have been fighting each other anyway, often in the name, if not the substance, of ideology. But there is a larger question. Even granting that a clearing of the intellectual atmosphere is necessary for more progress, how compelling a priority is the latter? Cannot Arab society survive well enough by muddling through? Does ideological confusion, or revolutionary half-heartedness, necessarily mean political instability? Perhaps the opposite is true.

There is no clear answer to this question. Yet we must bear in mind that by the time of Nasser's death, in Egypt, the leading Arab socialist state, the practical fruits of muddling through had been distinctly disappointing, both in international politics and in the domestic economy. Even if the 1967 war had never occurred, sooner or later the Malthusian economic situation was bound to make itself felt, and fundamental choices of priorities would have had to be made, between military and civilian expenditures, between welfare and investment, between egalitarian and privileged consumption patterns, between an Egypt-first and a Pan-Arab foreign policy—choices which Nasser's successors would have to face, but for which the Nasserist ideology simply never provided any guidelines. Under Nasser the ideology depended on constant promises of success, but the progressive decline toward failure and paralysis was less and less compatible with the regime's pretensions. From having set the standard for Arab nationalists everywhere, the regime and its message, by the time of Nasser's death in 1970, had become simply irrelevant. The 1967 disaster merely added an extra dimension of drama to this, and obscured the truth of the matter by seeming to offer an alibi for Egypt's domestic failures; for in the wake of the defeat, no one any longer expected miracles, and the regime thus gained a measure of reprieve. In retrospect, however, Nasser's Arab socialism may appear to many as a transitional phase in the modernization of Near Eastern political life, which contained the seeds of its eventual expiry all along. By the eve of the 1973 war, it seemed only a matter of time before Egypt would experience a substantial swing to either Right or Left.

[6] *Ibid.*, pp. 142–143.

The war was, of course, an important political success which bolstered the prospects of President Sadat and his Nasserist inheritance; and much could depend in the future on such possible windfalls as massive financial assistance from Saudi Arabia and other oil states, the reopening of the Suez Canal, etc., as well as on war or peace with Israel. What seems unlikely is that the ambiguous pattern of ideas and actions that Nasser had bequeathed to Egypt in the name of revolution could be revived as a basis for a dynamic social and political move-ment. And the chances appear strong that Egyptians will sooner or later feel a compelling need for a substitute.

In other Arab states that come under the Arab socialist label, the prospects are not necessarily the same. To be sure, successive regimes in Syria and Iraq also have been loud proclaimers of the gospel of Arab socialism, and imitators in many respects of Nasser and his system, if not altogether friendly to the Egyptians as such. They, like Nasser and his men, have been directly in conflict with Israel and might be thought to depend heavily for their political fortunes at home on their fate on the battlefield, where for geographical reasons the Libyan and Algerian leaders do not.

In several important respects the Syrians and Iraqis face a different situation with different strengths and weaknesses from those of Egypt. Their societies are far more ethnically diverse and politically disorderly; their economic potential in proportion to their populations is considerably greater, although this potential remains largely unrealized; their involvement with Israel, although a real and continuous problem, is relatively more peripheral in terms both of the energy and resources they must expend and the political strain that the post-1967 impasse seems to have put upon them; they are governed by branches of the Ba'ath party, with a select membership and, increasingly after the mid-1960s, a Marxist rather than Pan-Arab nationalist ideological outlook. Most significant, however, is the chronic problem of factionalism which has plagued Iraq and Syria ever since the independence of each, and which has produced coup after coup, while Egypt has displayed remarkable cohesion and stability despite all its problems.

Professor P. J. Vatikiotis suggests the nature of the problem.[7] With factional-ism as rife as that of Syria and Iraq, does it really make any difference what regime rules, and with what program and doctrine? After all, the ideology is but a fig leaf for the rulers of today, and they will be gone tomorrow. So his message seems to run. Whatever may be said about the Egyptians' difficulty of develop-ing a sense of priorities, it would appear that the Syrians and Iraqis face a more basic problem of developing a leadership stable enough to even be able to think seriously about priorities. Even those who are devoted to some clear policy

[7] See his chapter, "The Politics of the Fertile Crescent," in Paul Y. Hammond and Sidney S. Alexander, eds., *Political Dynamics in the Middle East* (New York: American Elsevier, 1972), pp. 225–263.

direction are at the mercy of their rivals in the struggle for power, and as they become inescapably preoccupied with their own problem of consolidating their position, they run the risk of losing sight of whatever sense of purpose they may originally have had. In a way, this appears to have been Nasser's problem. He became preoccupied, not so much with domestic but with foreign threats to his position, and wound up diverting his resources and energies into a disastrous series of external adventures. In another way, it was also the problem of the Palestinian Fedayeen: after 1967 they looked for a time like a truly innovative revolutionary force in Arab society (regardless of their military success against Israel), but ran aground in fighting amongst themselves and with the Jordanian, Lebanese, and other Arab governments. The first need for the Syrian and Iraqi Ba'athists, then, seems not to be more revolutionary but to find some formula for keeping harmony inside the regime.

Some may argue that in Syria, at least, this may be in the process of happening, not because of any magic formula but simply because every year since the Ba'ath came to power in 1963 has meant more irrevocable measures of economic and social change, industrialization, expansion of education and of the bureaucratic infrastructure of the state, and concentration of power within the ranks of Alawi army officers and a rising group of Marxist technocrats. Despite internal problems that produced an internal coup within the Ba'ath in 1966 and other shake-ups in 1969 and 1970, the fact remains that a party system of military and civilian leadership has survived to give continuity to Syrian politics. At the end of 1973, it has been in existence for almost eleven consecutive years—an unprecedented record in that country since its independence in 1945. Furthermore, the shake-up of November 1970 that removed President Atassi from power and brought Gen. Hafiz Asad to the fore seems to have ushered in a new sort of normality and rationality in the Syrian revolution, with greater concentration on internal development and less on external friction (leaving aside the special case of relations with Israel).

It may be premature to draw such optimistic conclusions about Syria. In the name of Ba'athist slogans, all sorts of further upheavals are still perfectly possible; and there is nothing to assure us that Alawi officers or Marxist civilian politicians will avoid quarreling among themselves, just because they have eliminated other rivals.[8]

In Iraq, the picture looks considerably less promising. For one thing, the problem of Kurdish autonomy looks basically insoluble, and a smoldering stalemate is probably the best that can be hoped for. The army is even more clique-ridden than in Syria, and different factions have gotten a good deal of

---

[8] For a first-class investigation of internal Syrian politics in the early and mid-1960s, see Itamar Rabinovich, *Syria Under the Ba'th 1963–66: The Army-Party Symbiosis* (New York: Wiley, 1973). I have tried to assess the post-1970 period in my essay "Hafiz Asad and the Changing Patterns of Syrian Politics," *International Journal* (Ottawa) 28 (Autumn 1973), 689–706.

each other's blood on their hands in the long chain of violent events occurring ever since the overthrow of the monarchy in 1958. In addition, Iraq has had serious border problems as well as a dangerous power rivalry with Iran which has focused on the question of future supremacy in the Gulf. Also, with a major oil industry, Iraq is enough of an economic prize for some outsiders to draw their rival attentions to a degree dangerous to herself. Somewhat as Syria in the 1950s was a kind of cockpit of inter-Arab and Great Power intrigues and power plays, very much to her own detriment, so Iraq may be destined for such a role in coming years.[9]

Given the problems of factionalism, as well as the proverbial Arab fascination with words and appearances and reputation, summed up so well by Sadek al-'Azm under the term *fahlawi*,[10] there is always the danger that the mere identification by such critics as al-'Azm of the problems, and the call for genuine revolutionary departures from debilitating habits and traditions, may prove to be little more than intellectual and psycho-political exercises, as short-cuts for actual deeds. ("Consider it done!" says al-'Azm's *fahlawi* prototype exuberantly, whenever asked to use his influence or get something accomplished for someone else.[11])

In summary, the leading Arab socialist states, to make a success of their revolutionary aspirations, appear to be in need of a combination of strong, assured, cohesive, sustained leadership on the one hand, and a clear sense of commitment, purpose and priorities (i.e., an effective ideology) on the other. But the achievement of such prerequisites is unlikely in the near future, for there is no movement committed to all of them that seems poised to make a bid for power anywhere. It is safer to assume that for a considerable time to come the Arab world will continue to be plagued with many of its familiar cultural and social ills: inoperable utopian modes of thought, a superficial mass politicization, factional strife, a preoccupation with images and reputations, bondage to conventionalism. What may be the first thing to give way, and it is already beginning to happen, is the middlist ideology of Nasserism or Arab socialism as a more or less formal and explicit gospel of success, and its replacement by alternative utopias of the Right and the Left; whether anything is done about it or not, growing numbers of people may come to assume that a move away from the center, and away from an atmosphere of inflated promises and expectations, is necessary. Whether such a shift of political outlook will really lead to any achievements, however, is another question. Rightists and leftists have each other to contend with in each Arab state, while dangers and opportunities in the neighborhood and abroad in the world may also be expected to compound the distractions for each of them.

---

[9] See the classic study of this by Patrick Seale, *The Struggle for Syria* (London: Oxford University Press, 1965).
[10] Al-'Azm, *Self-Criticism*, pp. 69–92.
[11] *Ibid.*, p. 80.

II. The Decline of the Myth of an Arab Prussia

The Arab League is approaching thirty years of age and, as one looks back on the kaleidescopic alignments and rivalries among the Arab states throughout this period, the most arresting fact seems to be the paradoxical combination of the Arabs' fascination with the idea of unity and their impotence to achieve it. We need not go into historical details here.[12] Perhaps, however, we are in a better position than a few years ago to draw a clear conclusion from all the events of the 1940s, fifties, and sixties: that no single Arab state can consistently control or even lead the others. The rulers of Syria, Iraq, and Saudi Arabia each at different times attempted to do so; after Nasser's rise in the early 1950s, and to some extent even before, the quest of Egypt for leadership became a more or less constant fact of inter-Arab life. But it was unsuccessful, despite all the natural advantages Egypt seemed to enjoy and the unusual personal qualities of Nasser himself; and the crisis of May 1967 can be regarded, in retrospect, as a desperate last major effort by Nasser to recapture the momentum of Pan-Arab leadership that he had gained, but then lost, in earlier years. With the Six-Day War the hope disappeared once and for all: not just Nasser's hope, but that of his vast following of Arabs whose utopian political outlook required a champion of the sort he seemed to be.

Since Nasser survived the war and continued to govern Egypt for over three additional years, his legend persisted in some measure also; and some of it was transferred to the Palestinian resistance movement and its leaders. But the blows dealt to the Fedayeen in Jordan, and Nasser's death immediately afterward, in September 1970, put an end to this; even the most deluded romantics had no choice thereafter but to put their hopes of Pan-Arab union and regeneration off to the indefinite future. We may sum up the import of all this by saying that what had happened was the dispelling of the myth of an "Arab Prussia": the Six-Day War underlined the fact that Egypt was not Prussia, and Nasser's death removed the prospective Arab Bismarck as well.

This being the case, what practical effect can we anticipate in the behavior and attitudes of the Arab regimes toward each other? Generally, it would seem that we are left with both a hope and a danger.

The hope is that with the shattering of the Pan-Arab Nasserist myth, Arab governments will each adopt a more modest, restrained, sober view of its own role. Not only will the Egyptian government lose interest in dominating a grand Pan-Arab coalition—even Nasser himself had moved well away from this before his death—but other regimes on the Left may perhaps survey the record and draw the conclusion that where Nasser failed they would be best advised not to try; while the conservative regimes such as Saudi Arabia and Jordan that in the

[12] I have dwelt on this subject in my chapter "Regional Arab Politics and the Conflict with Israel" (Hammond and Alexander, eds., *Political Dynamics*, pp. 31–68, as well as in the volume *The Arab Cold War: Gamal 'Abd al-Nasir and His Rivals, 1958–1970* (New York: Oxford University Press, 1971).

past have learned to fear and oppose Nasser and his partners, and have some-times made matters a good deal worse by their provocative counterattacks, may now feel more relaxed. The events of the fall of 1973 lend credibility to this thesis. Public preoccupation with issues of unity, which was largely debilitating since so little could really be accomplished, may mercifully recede. This may make it easier for various Arab states to practice diversity in their domestic politics and economics, their international alignments, and their positions vis-à-vis Israel. Shorn of the stakes of the power struggle, material cooperation among the Arab states in matters of trade, travel, communications, educational systems, law codes, and the like may become easier, so that in practice a greater degree of unity may accompany the abandonment of the mythology of full political union.

In the long run this sort of hope seems tenuous, however. It may be that no one will quite try to become another Nasser (although Colonel Qaddafi seems interested), but the fact remains that each Arab state shares common borders and at least some common problems with one or more others, and has to worry about its regional position, if not its weight, in the grand scales of Pan-Arabism. Thus, the Algerians may be expected to exchange the same wary attitudes with their Tunisian and Moroccan neighbors as before, and likewise the geographical groupings in northeast Africa, the Fertile Crescent, and the Arabian Peninsula are subject to local rivalries. Jordan's relations with Egypt, Syria, and Iraq declined badly for a time after Nasser's death; so did those between Saudi Arabia and the People's Republic of South Yemen; and the unhappy Palestinian exile population and its uncertain future continued to threaten the peace inside Lebanon and Jordan. Such problems can always recur.

Thus, we must fear that Nasser's disappearance means not only an end to Pan-Arab illusions, but also to the more mundane hope that he might at least be strong enough—as Bismarck was after 1871—to be a force for restraint among his neighbors through wise and adroit diplomacy, on at least an *ad hoc* basis, if not on the grand scale. He had, after all, reined in the Syrians during the 1958–1961 union; again, he had done so in the Arab summit meetings of 1964–1965; through his liaison with the Aref brothers in Iraq he had contributed to the peacefulness of Iraqi conduct from 1964–1967; in 1970 he had moderated the hot-headed approach of Qaddafi toward King Hussein. None of this would have been possible had Nasser not enjoyed the prestige of a revolutionary Pan-Arab hero. Granted that the Arab world could profit greatly from a respite from the overstimulation of Nasserism, can it do without Nasser?

Even if a general inter-Arab cold war is no longer to be feared, there remains the danger of a good deal of petty chaos over a long period of time, with a debilitating cumulative effect. Local issues will not disappear, nor will the need for outside economic and military aid and diplomatic patronage from one or another Great Power; nor, therefore, the prospect of opposition groups seeking the help of outsiders in seizing power by *coup d'état*. Nor will the problem of Israel completely dissolve, under the best of circumstances; and for some Arab states this issue must pose perennial dilemmas.

It is tempting to think that the Middle East would be better off, as would the Soviet Union and the United States, if the lines of clienthood and patronage were more sharply drawn, so that each Middle Eastern state were more wholly identified with and dependent upon one Great Power or the other—with Israel, Jordan, Lebanon, and Saudi Arabia on the one side, and Syria, Egypt, and Iraq on the other. With Egypt's growing tie to the Soviet Union, the departure of Nasser, and the suppression of the Fedayeen in Jordan, this pattern, in fact, appeared to be establishing itself, until the Egyptian dismissal of Soviet advisers in 1972. But such a formula is not really a promising one, for, with few exceptions, there is very little assurance that any given regime in this or that country will keep its grip on power, even with the enthusiastic support of its outside patron. America could not guarantee the internal *status quo* in Lebanon in 1958, still less today; nor can she control the succession in Jordan if King Hussein should disappear. Nor, conversely, can the Russians keep track of every concealed opposition faction in the armies of Syria, Iraq, or Egypt; Nasser himself, after all, could not keep a grip on the Syrian army in 1961 sufficiently to prevent a coup against the union. Furthermore, even without any new power struggles, it is always possible for regimes to undergo sharp changes in diplomatic direction if they see an opportunity to gain seomthing, as the inter-Arab realignment accompanying the 1973 war demonstrated. Thus, a well-delineated chessboard is not necessarily secure from sudden upsets.

Nonetheless, we should take pains to clarify one point. In a chaotic situation in which governments come and go by forceful means, the ongoing international problems of the Middle East (especially the Arab-Israeli problem) must be expected to work generally to the detriment of the more conservative and Western-affiliated regimes. This is partly because upheaval is no atmosphere in which conservatism can prosper, especially when it is a conservatism based on obsolescent cultural traditions, and partly because the resentment against Israel and her American patrons is deeply rooted and gathers strength as time passes and no progress toward resolving the conflict is made.

As this issue continues to strain Arab morale and undermine Arab political stability, therefore, the direction of the drift is likely to be consistently, perhaps acceleratedly, away from positions of rapport or dialogue with or dependence on the United States and toward greater hostility, unless genuine progress toward a settlement is made. The Libyan revolution of 1969 which overturned the monarchy and brought Colonel Qaddafi to power is a case in point: even when the new regime turns out to be militantly anti-Communist and puritanically Islamic in its ideology, it is at the same time unprecedentedly hostile toward the United States, on the explicit grounds of U.S. support for Israel. The United

States can take scant comfort from the divisions among Arab revolutionaries of the sort that pit the Qaddafis, Sadats, and Numeiris against the Communists in Sudan and the Ba'athists in Iraq, as happened in July 1971. And as the Arab oil boycott demonstrated in the fall of 1973, under the pressures of the conflict with Israel, even the most conservative Arab regimes were quite prepared to band together with the radicals in striking at vital American interests.

It seems likely that, for a long time to come, Egypt will continue to be the single most influential Arab state. Her large population and central location are permanent factors of preponderance; other present factors are of the sort that can only change slowly, if they change at all. These include Egypt's enormous margin over other Arab states in trained manpower, developed governmental machinery, cultural prestige, military establishment, industrialization and modern economic infrastructure, and established foreign connections. What the Egyptians lack is surplus cash, a charismatic leader, and insulation from the ambitions and rivalries of other nations stronger than themselves, including both Israel and the Great Powers. There being no early likelihood that these limitations will disappear, Egyptian pretensions to preeminent Pan-Arab leadership are probably not going to be revived. Certainly Egyptian public opinion does not need Pan-Arabism: Egyptians take it for granted that they are Egyptian before being Arab, and that a Pan-Arab policy like Nasser's is a calculated political strategy rather than an expression of sentiment. This sets them off sharply from Syrians, Iraqis, and other Arabs who lack independent traditions and consciousness of themselves as national societies.

There were some indications, if not very conclusive ones, that Nasser at the end of his life was looking for ways to extract Egypt gradually from its overcommitments and swing back to attention to domestic needs. His acceptance of the Rogers Plan and his professed willingness to reach a final settlement with Israel, over which he broke openly with the Palestinian guerrilla organizations and closed down their radio in Cairo in the summer of 1970, may have been no more than tactical devices aimed at getting the Israelis out of Sinai, in order to bounce back to his old position as the Pan-Arab champion and prime challenger of Israel. Many people in and out of Egypt thought otherwise, and were convinced Nasser was really looking for a way out.

But whatever his intentions, Nasser died; and Anwar al-Sadat, who succeeded him, was no Nasser. His power base inside Egypt was insecure, and when all the alternatives open to him in the subsequent three years are considered, Sadat's inclination to get Egypt off the hook with Israel—by war if necessary—and stabilize her relations with her fellow Arab states was surely considerable. Even if a settlement were somehow reached, disengagement from the outside world's quarrels would very likely continue to make sense to Sadat or any successor for a long time to come.

The main reason why it is unlikely that Sadat, even if fortified with a relatively favorable settlement with Israel, would plunge Egypt back into ambitious Pan-Arab or other adventures, is that neither in Egypt nor in neighboring Arab countries would he really find the necessary encouragement. Nasser had catered to an essentially non-Egyptian clientele when he played this game; the clientele was attached to Nasser's personal charisma, and is not freely transferable to the respectable but underwhelming figure of Anwar Sadat. Once rid of the Israelis, Egypt's number one foreign-policy concern would in all likelihood be to normalize her relations with the Great Powers and detach herself from regional and international controversies. It is clear that a great many Egyptians are tired of overextension and overinvolvement in international politics, and of the crushing economic burden that goes with it in the form of military budgets. Is another Nasser in the making in Egypt? The country simply will not be ready to give birth to him until after a considerable period of recuperation from the legacy of the previous Nasser.

In the absence of Egyptian hegemony, it is hardly likely that any other Arab state will succeed in taking her place. What could be its basis for doing so? Syria and Iraq, if joined together, would still have only half Egypt's population and a far less developed economy, although in sheer terms of physical resources their potential for development should be considerable, and Iraq's oil production provides an important supply of cash. One might imagine that were Syria to swing leftward to its pre-1970 position, then a Syro-Iraqi combination, perhaps together with South Yemen, could offer a common radical ideological front as a basis for forceful inter-Arab leadership. But leftist militancy is more likely to scare other Arab regimes off than to make them stand in line; and to judge by past patterns, it is doubtful whether Syria and Iraqi Ba'athists could keep their own combined internal house in order well enough to concentrate on foreign ventures, even if they were able to overcome their own mutual suspicions long enough to bring the union between themselves into being at all. Other Arab states may undergo changes that bring to power regimes of comparable ideologies—a modified Marxism-Leninism mixed with nationalism—but there is no reason to assume that this would lead to a wider merger with a pooled and stable leadership, capable of swinging the combined weight of the constituent members.

A monumental obstacle to Syrian and/or Iraqi Pan-Arab leadership is the existence of Jordan with its large Palestinian population. Much must depend on the three-cornered relationship between the Jordanian regime, the Palestinian resistance movement, and Israel. No Syrian or Iraqi regime with real ambitions can afford more than limited tolerance of the present Jordanian regime, which stands directly in the path of the fulfillment of the Palestinians' cause that purports to be so close to the Ba'thists' hearts. Yet until now King Hussein has been the buffer that none of the adjoining Arab radical states could afford to do without, though none could afford to admit the fact; for the alternative was bound to be very dangerous indeed. With or without the West Bank, a Jordan run by Palestinian militants would find it very difficult to avoid a heavy embroilment with Israel which would then threaten to result in a general escalation and a victory once more for Israeli arms so long as the Soviets remained nonbelligerent. What precise shape the confrontation might assume, and how the Israelis might follow through, one can only speculate upon; but whatever it was would certainly be incompatible with Syro-Iraqi Pan-Arab leadership. In short, then, while it is a constant possibility that the regime in Amman might suddenly change, what does not make sense is to project this possibility as a base for—or even as being compatible with—a successful union of radical regimes in the Fertile Crescent, able to provide credible inter-Arab leadership.

It remains for us to consider the possibility of Pan-Arab leadership coming not from the Left but the Right, with the supporting resource of oil wealth. By the eve of the 1973 war the challenge to Nasserist middlism from the Marxist Left had noticeably declined. Both in Egypt and Syria, leftists were demoralized and had been alternately co-opted and suppressed. The governments of these two countries had veered away from radical policies in domestic, inter-Arab, and international affairs. Sadat had ousted the Ali Sabry group in May 1971; a Marxist coup had been put down in the Sudan, with Egyptian help, in July; thousands of Soviet personnel were expelled from Egypt in July 1972; an agreement to unite Egypt and Libya was announced shortly afterward; student demonstrators and dissident intellectuals, many of them leftist, were disciplined early in 1973.

In many ways, Sadat himself projected an image of the leader of a comfortable bourgeois regime, mixed with an earthy peasant conservatism. He seemed equally at home hobnobbing with village smallholders, American diplomats, and King Faisal. To be sure, he was under inescapable pressure by virtue of the continuing presence of Israel along the Suez Canal, and his continual threats of renewed warfare, which stirred a rising wave of derision among his countrymen, seemed to bespeak a sense of desperation for the future of his regime.

The primary ideological challenge to Sadat's Nasserist legacy, during the last year or so before the 1973 war, took the form of the Islamic fundamentalist message represented by Col. Mu'ammar al-Qaddafi. While Qaddafi was scorned by Cairo's sophisticates, with his puritanical record in Libya and his talk of a society governed by the Koran, he held a crucial advantage, both among ordinary citizens of Egypt and other Arab countries and potentially even among the better-educated classes who were becoming uneasy with the political and social impasse that Nasserism has led them to: the power of zealous conviction, attached to a cultural force that was indisputably and authentically Arab.

Thus, Qaddafi represented far more than the power of Libyan money in inter-Arab affairs; and despite the paucity of his other political resources— Libya's small population, fledgling armed forces, undeveloped bureaucracy, and sparse reserve of skilled manpower—it was no simple matter for Sadat or other Arab leaders to try to manipulate or even ignore him. Those who wondered why the Egyptians did not simply consummate the full union with Libya demanded by Qaddafi, and then walk in and help themselves to her oil wealth, brushing aside the upstart young colonel in the process, failed to take account of the primordial sentiment that he embodied. Furthermore, for all his provinciality, Qaddafi brought to bear on Sadat and others a remarkable force of personality and intellect.

Presumably, Qaddafi was interested in union with Egypt because he realized that there was little he could accomplish without the geographic, cultural, military, and human base that she could provide. By all reports, there was little love lost between him and Sadat throughout their extended contacts from 1971 through August 1973. Eventually, Sadat was able to outmaneuver him, and to arrive at the projected date of union on September 1 without having to go through with it, but only after the most elaborate campaign of inter-Arab diplomatic juggling and fence-mending, by which he secured the support of Saudi Arabia, Syria, and Jordan.

Thus, Sadat succeeded in neutralizing Libyan influence in Egyptian affairs by swinging to Quaddafi's chief Arab rival, the arch-conservative Faisal; and when the October war was launched, it became clear that Sadat had shut Qaddafi out while laying his plans in consultation with his other Arab partners. The war was a heavy blow to Qaddafi's position, for it left him standing impotently on the sidelines, while cementing broad support from other Arab states, including the most conservative, for Egypt and Syria. Hence it had the effect of discrediting the thesis that the post-Nasserist system was vulnerable to right-wing as well as left-wing militancy. But for how long? This would depend on a host of domestic and external circumstances: the state of the Egyptian economy, Sadat's and Asad's success or failure in negotiating Israeli military withdrawals, and, as a background factor, the course of Faisal's relations with the United States in the aftermath of the oil boycott.

In large measure the events of fall 1973 represented a surprising success for King Faisal in Arab affairs: surprising, not only because at no time in the preceding twenty years had Saudi Arabia attained such ascendancy, but also because few observers had imagined that it was possible. To be sure, the Saudi government was rich, and Faisal himself, like his father King Abdul Aziz (though unlike his brother King Saud), was universally recognized as a consummate political practitioner. Yet, amidst the turbulent atmosphere of social, cultural, and political progressivism that marked the Arab world in Nasser's time, what Faisal represented seemed rather irrelevant—a holding action for the conservative backwaters of Arab society, doomed to give way in the long run and certainly incapable of stirring the enthusiasm of the rising secular generation who were supposed to count. By his adroitness and capitalization on Nasser's mistakes,

Faisal survived, and, indeed, in the aftermath of the 1967 war he looked impressively secure; Egypt, after all, now depended heavily on Saudi financial subsidies. But inter-Arab leadership was presumably something else again.

Two considerations in 1973 made an important difference. One was the Egyptian need to find a counterweight to Qaddafi's militancy, as already mentioned. In this respect access to Saudi money was, of course, important, since to some extent the Egyptian government was in the position of renouncing Libyan money by virtue of renouncing the plan for union. But beyond this, Faisal as a tested, respected, independent statesman was being invoked as an ally, carrying with him the great weight of Arab-Islamic orthodoxy and conservatism that still pervaded the outlook of the bulk of Egyptian and Arab society. In this role Faisal carried more authority than, say, the Sheikh of Kuwait would have done, while on the other side he should by no means be confused with Qaddafi, a fellow devotee of Islamic values and symbols but in a very different key; for Qaddafi signified radical fundamentalism implying revolutionary upheaval, while Faisal signified prudence, caution, order, and continuity.

The other new consideration that enhanced Faisal's role in 1973 was that his country's status as an oil producer had reached a point of maturation that enabled him for the first time to wield the oil weapon with some authority against the United States and its industrial partners, and thus—as much the largest Arab producer—to provide the political muscle on which other Arab states depended for leverage against Israel. Saudi oil income and financial reserves had by now climbed well into the billions; like other producers, her relations with the oil companies had turned strongly in her favor, especially since the Teheran agreements of 1971; a small but growing class of technically sophisticated men had become available to the Saudi government, typified by the Minister for Petroleum Affairs Sheikh Ahmad Zaki Yamani, to deal with Western companies and governments as professional equals. Egyptians and Syrians, together with Westerners, could no longer dismiss the Saudis as barefoot boys in Cadillacs.

With the 1973 war, while Sadat's own reputation was obviously enhanced in the Arab arena, and while it would be up to him to take the overt lead in subsequent dealings with Israel, it became clear at the same time that King Faisal had acquired an unprecedentedly potent background role as a broker, both with the United States and among the Arabs themselves.

What remained to be seen, at the end of 1973, was the role of Saudi money and diplomacy in Arab society, looking beyond success or failure of the short-term effort to negotiate an acceptable settlement with Israel. Money was bound to count, but money alone would not assure the solution of underlying problems in the poorer, more populous Arab countries struggling with the pains and mysteries of making their own way in the contemporary world; and Saudi Arabia herself, as a relatively insulated and archaic society, could scarcely provide a model. Indeed, jolting political changes within her own territory could not be excluded after the departure of Faisal from the scene.

III. The Arabs and Israel: Convergent Interests in a Settlement?

No one can doubt that the course of the Arab-Israeli conflict over the next decade or two will depend in important respects on the actions of the Soviet Union and the United States, but the central fact remains that the conflict has its own local dynamics in the attitudes and actions of the parties themselves. The outside patrons of the parties can perhaps set limits to their clients' behavior, by a variety of inducements, admonitions, assurances, and incitements; but they cannot determine how the parties will identify their own interests or how they will respond to each other. Again, the superpowers, in their efforts to manipulate the local situation, are primarily motivated by matters that transcend the regional issues or are even irrelevant to them, and the issues themselves may therefore look highly parochial to the strategists in Moscow and Washington. But these same issues mean everything in the Middle East, and it is, after all, the Middle Easterners on their own home ground who will wind up making war or peace.

Logically, this seems an obvious point; yet this writer is struck by the implicit tendency of many American foreign-policy analysts to see the Arab-Israeli problem simply as a test of strength between Soviet and American proxies. Thus, the supposed central issue becomes whether the Soviet Union will "neutralize the Sixth Fleet" or "outflank NATO" through the acquisition of air and naval bases in Egypt and Syria, and whether Israeli military strength will serve to "interdict" such moves. From there, one moves on unconsciously toward the false conclusion that it is the growing Soviet military presence, and Soviet strategic designs, that underlie the Arab-Israeli conflict itself in the first place, and constitute the chief obstacle to a solution. Seen in this light, the security of Israel becomes a matter of basic American strategic interest rather than simply human sympathy and concern; and with this transition, the particular issues between Israelis and Arabs cease to matter very much, the important assumption being, that as the Israelis look after their own interests, they serve American ones in the process. Peace will come, according to this perspective, when the Soviets and their Arab protégés realize that Israel cannot be destroyed.

The above lines may appear caricaturized to some, yet, even at some sophisticated levels in Washington and in the academic world, they describe the essentials of established attitudes—attitudes which, in fact, have underlain two decades of American foreign-policy blunders in the Middle East in which cold war fixations distorted the perception of what the local problems were all about. We need to get back to ground level in our look at the Arab-Israeli problem, and remind ourselves that the parties involved are not, and do not think of themselves as being or behave as, representatives of Great Power interests. Furthermore, on both sides of the conflict they are diverse and complicated peoples who cannot be looked upon for purposes of American strategic forecasting and policy planning simply as homogeneous units with single-minded attitudes.

There are more than two sides in the struggle, and more than one issue. The question of Israel's right to exist is undoubtedly the central issue for many people both in Israel and in Arab lands, but by no means is this the issue for everyone, and it must be seen in a context of several other concerns. For many Arabs, what kind of Israeli state is tolerable—and for many Israelis, what kind of state is worth having—is the crucial question. What borders, what population, what internal social and political system, what relationship to Jews elsewhere are all important components of this question. Again, if Israel exists but is unrecognized and ostracized—but unmolested—by her neighbors, and in turn she ignores them, to whom would or would not this state of affairs be acceptable? What about the Palestinians? Can the existence of an Israel somehow be reconciled with the existence of a Palestine? And what about the Arab regimes in Egypt, Syria, Jordan, and elsewhere; to what extent are their internal character and their interrelationships within the Arab world matters which Israelis consider of concern to themselves and compatible with their own interests?[13]

In searching for common denominators we may find that some significant segments of official and unofficial opinion in both Israeli and Arab society at various times in the past have been receptive toward certain compromise formulas, but have been consistently upstaged, outbid, or discredited by more militant elements among their own compatriots, spurned by leaders on the other side at the moment their hand was extended, or let down by mishandling on the part of outside powers. These problems are most drastic on the Arab side, given the Arab reluctance to acquiesce in the series of *faits accomplis* that have led to the present state of affairs; the "moderate" Arab, after all, is in the nature of the case a "defeatist," whereas the "moderate" Israeli is simply in favor of giving back relatively more territory in exchange for relatively fewer assurances of peace, and is, therefore, a mini-annexationist ("a little peace and a little annexation," as satirists have said of Mapam's position, for instance).[14] But the problems are no less real and may have been equally decisive on the Israeli

---

[13] Premier Ben-Gurion told the Knesset on April 2, 1957, after the Sinai campaign, "This campaign diminished the stature of the Egyptian dictator and I do not want you or the entire people to underestimate the importance of this fact. As one of those persons who receive their salaries for looking after our security . . . I always feared that a personality might rise such as arose among the Arab rulers in the seventh century or like him [Kemal Ataturk] who arose in Turkey in the First World War. He raised their spirits, changed their character, and turned them into a fighting nation. There was and still is a danger that Nasser is this man." (Quoted in Kennett Love, *Suez: The Twice-Fought War* [New York: McGraw-Hill, 1969], p. 676.)

[14] Abraham S. Becker, *Israel and the Palestinian Occupied Territories: Military-Political Issues in the Debate* (Santa Monica, Calif.: The Rand Corporation, December 1971), R-882-ISA, p. 55.

side—as a look at the differences between Ben-Gurion and Sharett in the 1950s may suggest; and in the future this may be the case again.

Given the fact that the Arabs have consistently been the losers in the conflict, and that it is their acceptance of her existence that is the one thing that Israel has been unable thus far to obtain, it seems obvious we should not always have asked simply, "Are the Arabs ready to make peace?" which is an artificially one-dimensional question, but rather, "What would it take, and what must be done, to obtain a sufficient measure of acceptance of Israel's existence from a sufficient number of Arabs to achieve at least a provisional settlement and thereby, for the first time, to enable time to work in favor of peace?" This is essentially the question that Professor Alexander has posed in his excellent Introduction to *Political Dynamics in the Middle East*[15] ; and as he makes clear, what is needed is not simply to rely on the Arabs' presumed need to concentrate on their own domestic problems but to offer them some measure of satisfaction of their political demands vis-à-vis Israel. Whether Egypt's number one priority really has been a "quest for dignity" as Alexander asserts, or (a subtle but important difference) a quest for prestige need not detain us here. The point is that progress toward peace requires a mutual accommodation of political claims, including Arab claims as well as Israeli ones, and this should not be dismissed on the specious grounds that the only real Arab claim is for Israel's liquidation. Again, Alexander is perceptive in pointing out the falsity of the Israelis' supposition after 1967 that they had to choose between seeking "real peace" and "safety first," which was, as he says, "a 'cop-out,' an avoidance of the genuine problems of decision," summed up in the Israeli slogan "no other way."[16]

From 1948 to the war of 1973, successive Israeli governments sought consistently to cash in on the particular advantage they held—in military superiority—and to purchase a full-scale peace agreement based more or less on the territorial and political *status quo*. Failing that, they preferred simply to hold on to their military superiority. The diplomatic exchanges from 1967–1973 were the latest rerun of this pattern. Forceful Israeli actions in the past—border raids and reprisals, the Sinai sampaign, the Six-Day War itself—had served as attempts to force the issue of peace, to bring Arab governments to the realization that keeping the struggle open was dangerous to themselves, and that they could not afford to postpone a peace settlement; when these actions failed to achieve that purpose, the Israeli assessment was to the effect that this was an Arab problem alone.

The policy which Alexander sums up as a cop-out was by no means a post-1967 innovation. The question after the 1973 war, which followed a different pattern from previous ones, is whether this Israeli approach may change.

[15] Hammond and Alexander, eds., *Political Dynamics.* See especially p. xxvii.
[16] *Ibid.*, p. xx.

Israel's effort to gain the desired political benefits from her military superiority was like a currency transaction. Her superiority appeared to her to be hard currency, by all rights freely convertible at face value, whereas in actuality it was quite soft, exchangeable only at a significant discount. The Arab states found that they could get along—not comfortably, but tolerably well—without the transaction, and could thus avoid the pain of debating among themselves whether, even at a discount and, if so, how much of one, they should contemplate bargaining with Israel at all. What they all held in common was a refusal to recognize Israel's armed strength at full face value, that is, as decisive in itself. To reverse a widespread American cliché, if there was one thing the Arabs did not "understand" it was force.

It does not seem likely that any particular developments we can anticipate within Arab society will alter this situation, except to harden it, if the conflict remains open. Even before the 1973 war arrived to improve Arab morale, the long succession of Arab military and political failures in the face of the Zionist movement—reaching back well before the creation of the Jewish state—had left them as well placed as ever to resist a settlement based on abandonment of all their claims. In this historical perspective, it is now surely late in the day to persist in the illusion that a little more time will work in favor of making the Arabs conclude that they have no alternative to peace on whatever terms they can get. In the past, their adamant political position has not been based on strength and prosperity but on weakness and confusion and on the continuing practical and psychological ability to say no as long as saying yes offered no compensatory recovery of past losses. For Israel in this situation, inflicting military defeats on the Arabs was like punching a pillow; the Arabs could continue to absorb successive defeats without result.

All this is not to say that the Arabs, being able to resist a settlement on the terms offered on Israel, see no benefit in a settlement on terms more favorable to themselves. For despite its demonstrated ability to survive defeats, Arab society at large has paid a heavy price for the continuation of the conflict, and the price could well get worse. This price may perhaps best be described, not in terms of material cost (military expenditures, lives lost, refugees) but in terms of the unsettling effects on the psychological, social, and political order, which have been considerable indeed and have served to exacerbate difficulties which each of Israel's Arab neighbors was bound to be faced with in any case.

The segment of Arab opinion which has always spurned discussion of a compromise settlement has consistently spoken with the loudest voice, and, indeed, on a number of critical occasions, has intimidated more moderate elements from advancing their own views and initiatives effectively. This, however, is but a natural reflection of the unequal bargaining position vis-à-vis Israel in which the Arabs have long found themselves; for terms of settlement that would appeal to the sense of propriety and self-respect of even the most conciliatory Arab elements have not been available. Consequently, the moderates have tended to find it unprofitable to push arguments in favor of concessions in return for only hypothetical gains, and so appear as dupes, faint-hearts, or worse; while the more passive and impressionable mass of opinion is readily swung by default to the view that the stakes of the struggle with Israel must be total, no intermediate set of stakes being clearly visible to them as a live option. Needless to say, major political careers may be made by capitalizing on this state of affairs.

Conversely, it remains to be seen what shift of opinion would be generated if international diplomacy were to bring to the surface a genuine alternative. Were such an alternative to entail, in significant measure, the symbols of requitement of longstanding Arab grievances—notably, the restoration of national territories, some formula recognizing in principle the entitlement of Palestinians to redress of personal loss and hardship, recognition of the Palestinians' national character and right of self-determination—then the potential adjustment of Arab political opinion to new realities would for the first time be put to the test, and an opportunity for new political careers capitalizing on new public attitudes would become possible. If this last notion is too sanguine, we may at least hope for a significant psychological disengagement from the treadmill of conflict-oriented attitudes, thus providing valuable time for national leaders seeking to shore up their societies against the internal threats of disintegration that confront them.

Judging by the circumstances surrounding the 1973 war and its immediate aftermath, the leaders of Egypt and Syria appear to have viewed it as an opportunity to break the diplomatic logjam and attain a bargaining position in which the new alternative to which we have referred could become a live option. The generating of new pressures on the United States, Western Europe, and Japan to apply pressure in turn on Israel to modify her position was the most obvious component of this strategy; the effort to give maximum exposure to Israel's isolation, vulnerability, and dependence on external support—summed up as exploding the myth of Israeli invincibility—was another.

Equally important, however, was the contribution the war made to overcoming the converse myth of Arab impotence, or, as some have termed it, the Arab "Mickey Mouse complex." Of course, a logical case may be made that the bolstering of Arab self-confidence will simply mean the deepening of their intransigence, with the militants now arguing that no compromise is necessary since the tide is turning in the Arabs' favor and time is on their side. This analysis is a simple extension of the logic followed by the Israeli government since 1948 to which we have alluded above, in its effort to translate military superiority into a favorable settlement; and it is unconvincing for the same reasons. If repeated confirmations of Arab weakness did not induce a readiness on their part to cut their losses by making a sacrificial peace, we may conversely doubt that indications of growing strength will induce them to press indefinitely for total victory. On the contrary, it may be at least as plausibly supposed that with a new sense of something more closely approaching bargaining parity, the psychological ground on the Arab side may now be better prepared than before for a serious negotiation. Among both Arabs and Israelis the logic of psychology has been more fundamental than the logic of military power in explaining the persistence of the conflict for the past quarter of a century; were the reverse the case, it would have been settled long ago.

In December 1973, however, it is not yet certain that the strengthening of the Arab bargaining position is as significant as what meets the eye. Materially, it depends heavily on the impact of the oil weapon on American diplomacy and the prospect of persuading the United States to make decisive changes in the character and extent of its support of Israel. What looks like a highly promising development from the Arab side may substantially dissolve in time, either because, for one reason or another, the oil weapon does not remain a usable or effective device long enough, or because, whatever the American policy, Israel finds it possible and desirable to stick to her previous position. In these circumstances, the pre-1973 impasse may reassert itself.

Should this happen, what may change with time is not the Arabs' inability to withstand Israel's insistence on her own terms but the Arab interest in any terms at all. Until the energy crisis and the oil boycott were upon us, there seemed reason to wonder if the Arab interest in a settlement had not virtually disappeared already, for lack of any visible prospects of American willingness to induce changes in Israel's posture. The failure of the Rogers Plan and the proposed Suez Canal interim settlement in 1970–1971, and the futility of Egypt's expulsion of Soviet forces in 1972, had left President Sadat looking rather gullible, and this result did not encourage further efforts by Arab governments to stick their necks out in favor of diplomacy. If, after additional diplomatic failures following the 1973 war, a new impasse sets in, it is possible that each Arab regime will simply adjust itself to the practical ways of coping indefinitely with the *status quo,* taking for their model the stance habitually taken in the years before 1973 by Syria: no talks, even with intermediaries; verbal commitment to a Palestinian people's war of national liberation; an ongoing reliance on the USSR for military and diplomatic assistance; an occasional small-scale provocation of Israel (and absorption of Israeli retaliation) for the sake of credibility; and not much else. Long-term financial underwriting from one or another of the oil states, perhaps Libya if not Saudi Arabia, would keep the Syrian and Egyptian defense budgets going. Such a state of affairs could quite conceivably persist for a very long time. (It is a neat minor irony that the Ba'ath regime in Damascus, whose overthrow was alleged by Nasser and other Arabs to be Israel's objective in the 1967 crisis, was still surviving six years later, under the leadership of none other than the man who had been Minister of Defense in 1967.) Yet, however stable this prospect on the local conflict level, it certainly would not augur well for the internal health of Arab national regimes and societies, nor for the normalization of their relations with Israel's friends in the outside world.

This proposition glosses over many things, notably the future of Jordan, Lebanon, and the Fedayeen organizations. It may be argued that the Syrian government's posture from 1967–1973 was made much easier by the fact that in compensation for its own quiescence it was able to cheer on the Palestinians who were active from inside Lebanese and Jordanian territory; and with Hussein's suppression of the Fedayeen in Jordan, he could be castigated and boycotted as a convenient scapegoat. If we imagine Jordan and Lebanon, as well as Egypt, coming under the rule of radicals of the Syrian stamp, so that Israel were entirely surrounded by such regimes, presumably one or more of them would have to give the Fedayeen a fairly free hand—and thereby invite a really heavy Israeli response—or else they would have to clamp down on the Fedayeen and invite an open political conflict with the latter that could discredit these regimes' claims to revolutionary legitimacy.

But all this is not necessarily the case. In a prolonged situation of open confrontation between the Israeli armed forces and Fedayeen units in Syria, Lebanon, and Jordan, an effective stalemate would be likely to develop sooner or later. The military potential of the Fedayeen is limited, while in the face of prospective problems of all sorts there is also an inhibition in Israel against invading and occupying more territory. Even before Hussein repressed the Fedayeen in September 1970, the Israelis had effectively tightened their security on the Jordan River, and the fighting between them and the Fedayeen had leveled off; Hussein may have eased Israel's problem as a more radical Arab leader would not, but the Fedayeen had probably already passed their peak as a security challenge to Israel. In the future, the Fedayeen, like the radical regimes we are imagining, may continue to exist as a movement, making periodic gestures of credibility and preaching the rejection of all compromise, but becoming more and more a digested element of the *status quo.* In short, while the Palestinians may have been the forgotten men of the conflict in the past, if the conflict remains open there is no great reason to assume they are the wave of the future.

Turning now to Israel's position, it is important again to distinguish the most immediate impact of the 1973 war from the longer-term considerations that the war may have brought to light but which have been implicit for some time already. Like the Arabs, Israelis have grown accustomed to viewing the conflict in stereotypic and symbolic terms, bringing an acute concern for "security" to bear alongside the Arab concern for "justice." It might be remarked that somewhat as Arabs look for psychological restitution from abroad as well as from Israel—that is, that their hostilities have long been kindled as much by what they perceive as the contemptuous insouciance of the Western world as by what they view as Israeli ruthlessness—so Israeli's sense of insecurity extends to factors well beyond the threat posed by neighboring Arabs.

The so-called holocaust complex is a familiar element, but there is much else besides. As a minor point one might speculate, for instance, about the effects of the sense of insularity and claustrophobia in a small country with closed borders and heavily dependent on air transport, reflected not only in the urge to travel abroad, but also in the euphoria produced among Israelis by the *de facto* territorial expansion that followed the 1967 war. What is clearly of major importance, however, is the degree of Israel's material and moral dependence on the external world, a dependence that was dramatized by the need for a massive transfusion of American arms and money in October 1973 and the equally massive rise in Israeli taxation, but which had always been at least subconsciously perceived in Israel as a fundamental reality. What was exploded for Israelis in the October war may not have been so much a myth of invincibility— the military setback, after all, was only of a few days' duration, and Israel had suffered relatively heavy casualties in previous conflicts—as a complacent sense of self-sufficiency, to the effect that Israel's future lay in her own hands. Vague anxieties in the past that American national interests might diverge from Israel's and that American support might dwindle, now became more immediate and real.

Concomitantly, the longstanding notion that Arab intransigence constituted an Arab rather than an Israeli problem demanded a rethinking. This was not because the perception of the intransigence itself had changed (on the contrary, to judge from many reports, this perception was considerably strengthened within the Israeli public, causing the disillusionment of many an erstwhile dove).[17] But Arab claims on Israel had now, by virtue of the oil weapon, become a worldwide, and notably an American concern, and consequently also an Israeli one, so that the need for a negotiated settlement, even on terms that had attracted little favor in Israel before the war, now became eligible for serious consideration. The prospect of facing not simply the degree of international diplomatic isolation of the previous few years but, additionally, an open breach with the United States, coupled with a steeply rising defense budget and a continuing partial mobilization, could not be reconciled with a long-term negotiating stalemate with the Arabs.

On the other hand, we have already remarked that the shift in the American position may not prove to be as considerable or as lasting as the Arabs hoped, in which case the possibility of a renewed stalemate may resurface, with conditions

[17] See, for example, Amnon Rubinstein, "The Israelis: No More Doves," *The New York Times Magazine,* 21 October 1973. See also the statement of a group of Israeli professors of October 1973 in support of the government and condemning the Syrian-Egyptian attack, reprinted in *New Outlook* (Oct.–Nov. 1973) pp. 24–25. "The real issue today, as it was in 1967," declared the professors, "is the determination by Egypt and Syria to destroy Israel."

along the cease-fire lines returning eventually to something like the previous equilibrium. While this turn of events may relieve Israel of the prospect of a diplomatic crisis, in time it is likely to prove increasingly troublesome to her in other ways.

Domestic social discontent may be one such problem. Until now, and perhaps in some limited ways in the future, the persistence of the conflict with the Arabs has been a presumptive lubricant of social harmony in Israel among different economic classes and national origin groups. As these two categories broadly coincide, with Oriental Jews constituting the bulk of the poorer segment of society, the long-term potentialities for serious friction on a large scale, on a political as well as a social level, cannot be dismissed. This is often posed in some quarters as one of the dangers if peace should break out, but meanwhile a more real danger may arise in precisely opposite circumstances. Continuing conflict with the Arabs means the indefinite maintenance of a costly military budget and a squeeze on the attention and the money the government can afford to devote to problems of health, education, welfare, housing, and urban development.

Professor Nadav Safran, writing a few years ago, acknowledged the argument that this situation could "trigger social conflicts that could stimulate the latent communal problem, causing grave intercommunal strife. The necessary counter-measures might involve a combination of formal and informal repression and jingoistic propaganda that would generate an oppressive, intolerant, embattled atmosphere in the country." But he went on to dismiss such fears, arguing, on the one hand, that perhaps half the increase in the military budget in the first few years after 1967 had been due to investment in a domestic weapons-production capacity and that, therefore, the increase would level off, and, on the other hand, that the 1967 war somehow "accomplished a near miracle in bridging the subjective gap" between Israelis of European and Oriental origin.[18] These conclusions do not today appear very satisfactory. Even disregarding the industrial investment component of the defense budget increases, there remained plenty of room for further rises up to 1973 and beyond, if for no other reason than the continuous increase in weapons sophistication; and whatever euphoria Europeans and Orientals may have shared as a result of the Six-Day War, it would be difficult to imagine that such an experience could reverse the whole dynamics of a social problem whose objective material foundations are so substantial. A tradeoff may make some sense part of the time—more wars as a compensation for less welfare, more psychological equality in the trenches in place of more material equality at home—but in the long run this is artificial. It brings to mind the false hope entertained in the United States in the 1960s that better race relations were being forged by the soldiers in Vietnam.

Added to this is the somewhat related problem of what to do with the

[18] "Israel's Internal Politics and Foreign Policy," in Hammond and Alexander, eds., *Political Dynamics*, pp. 191–192.

population of the occupied territories as the stalemate wears on; for as time drags out in Gaza and the West Bank, and the Israeli occupation takes on an air of permanence, the denial of civil and political rights to a million or more Arab inhabitants, and of unimpeded access between them and refugee Palestinians in the outside world, may become more and more anomalous. The difficulties that can arise locally for Israel in policing the occupied territories—accumulating petty grievances, equally petty punitive actions, occasional scandals over abuses of authority, eventually, perhaps, culminating in campaigns of passive resistance—may be much less dramatic but, eventually, much more damaging to Israel's position than the problem of combating Fedayeen infiltrators and airline terrorists, who, after all, are fair game for whatever armed force Israel can bring to bear. Of course, the two problems may in time feed on each other, which could create a nightmarish situation; but even assuming that the Fedayeen are kept under reasonable control, the occupation problem alone may prove bad enough.

Eventually, the development of such situations must pose a serious challenge to the liberal democratic political conscience in Israel; to a small extent this has already begun to happen. It is also potentially harmful to Israel's reputation abroad. In conjunction with the social tensions within Israel's own Jewish population, one can imagine a day in the future in which foreign and domestic critics alike will compare the respective positions of European Jews, Oriental Jews, and Palestinian Arabs in Israel and the occupied territories with whites, coloreds, and blacks in South Africa. Justified or not, accusations of this sort would be a heavy burden for a country as dependent as Israel is on the high morale of its citizens and of its foreign supporters. Beyond the enthusiasm and financial support of European and American Jewry, equally important to Israel is the general attitude of protective sympathy and benevolence of non-Jewish opinion and of the governments who represent them, especially in an age in which the voices of Europe, Africa, and Asia, alongside the Soviet bloc, are becoming increasingly unfriendly. To be sure, a wave of misgivings among some of Israel's traditional friends and supporters would not be the end of the world for her, and might fall short of forcing her against her own wishes to change her basic policies toward the Arab world. Even countries as diplomatically isolated and unpopular in the world as South Africa and Rhodesia are today still doing very nicely. Many Israelis, however, do not wish to see Israel become a South Africa or a Rhodesia, and would regard evolving in such a direction as a very high price to pay for whatever security the occupied territories provided.

These are some of the considerations that lead one to wonder if Israel may find, even if the neighboring Arab states prove powerless to challenge her more effectively than they have thus far, that she has painted herself into a corner and that, as her own power and territory have expanded, she has become increasingly isolated in the world. In spite of her military preponderance, she may conclude belatedly that she is in as great a need of a compromise settlement with Egypt, Syria and Jordan—and, through them, with the Palestinians—as they with her. In that case, the question of what kind of settlement the various Arab elements would contemplate will for the first time acquire a really practical importance.

PART III

The Superpowers
in the Arab-Israeli Conflict, 1970-1973

Abraham S. Becker

To those who had begun to believe in the final demise of the cold war after the Moscow and Washington summit meetings of 1972–1973, Soviet behavior in October 1973 came as a shock. Doubts of the continued viability of the Soviet-American détente were widespread, and the Nixon Administration was pressed on numerous occasions to clarify its understanding of the state of relations with the USSR. Some say that détente has been confused with entente in the public mind. Others insist that it is not just in the public mind that the confusion has occurred. The Nixon Administration has asserted that it will not be satisfied with "selective détente," but it is not entirely clear whether it believes the events of October fall under that heading.

The argument of Part III is that if the pattern of Soviet-American relations in the Middle East in earlier years is defined as détente, then the term also characterizes superpower interactions during October 1973. The actions of Moscow (and of Washington, too) in the fall of 1973 are not inconsistent with behavior patterns in previous crises since the Six-Day War; indeed, the October war events confirm the generalizations derived from examination of the record of superpower interaction in the last three or four years. To this observer, rethinking the state of Great Power involvement in the Arab-Israeli conflict as 1973 ends, it seems striking how much we still stand in the shadow of the events of 1970; how significant the events of that drama-filled year were in illuminating relationships among the major protagonists.

Therefore, I will begin with a review of some highlights of the approximately fourteen-month period from December 1969 to February 1971, which, for brevity's sake, is designated simply, "1970." The review sets the stage for discussion of the central issues, the evolving rules of Soviet-American military interaction and the efforts of both superpowers to avoid mutual military confrontation. A concluding section considers prospects in the Middle East after the October war.

Some notable topics are ignored or mentioned only briefly; in particular, the Two- and Four-Power negotiations on the Middle East in 1969–1970, and the internal components of both U.S. and Soviet policy in the region. The first omission is probably of small consequence but the latter set of issues cannot be easily dismissed. I am inclined to the view that the economic dimension of Soviet Middle Eastern policy in this period is a negligible factor, that neither the costs of the Soviet regional operation[1] nor the well-known difficulties of the Soviet domestic economy have played a significant role in shaping Soviet Middle East policy.[2] However, the absence of any discussion of Soviet domestic politi-

[1] See Gur Ofer, "The Economic Burden of Soviet Involvement in the Middle East", *Soviet Studies* 24 (no. 3, Jan. 1973):329–347. Also, J. R. Carter, *The Net Cost of Soviet Foreign Aid* (New York: Praeger, 1971).

[2] On the role of oil in Soviet policy, see A. S. Becker, "Oil and the Persian Gulf in Soviet Policy in the 1970s", in Michel Confino and Shimon Shamir, eds., *The USSR and the Middle East* (Jerusalem: Israel Univer. Press, 1973).

cal considerations—or of their American counterparts—and their effects on foreign policy is undoubtedly a limitation of the discussion. I can only point to other limitations—of space, time, and my own talent—that compel me to refrain from attempting to repair the gap.

II. The Long Shadow of 1970

As 1969 drew to a close, Nasser's intermittent War of Attrition at the Suez Canal had been in progress for nine months. A new American administration, concerned that the Middle Eastern powder keg might be ignited momentarily, made public in December a set of proposals for settlement of the conflict, the so-called Rogers Plan, that provided for almost complete Israeli withdrawal from Sinai and the West Bank. The proposals were met by a storm of denunciation in Israel and little overt support in the Arab world. Moreover, they were soon overwhelmed by a rapid escalation of Soviet involvement.

January 1970 saw the inauguration of Israeli air strikes into the heart of Egypt in response to Egyptian attacks along the canal. Nasser appealed to Moscow for help and in February and March Soviet technicians set up a surface-to-air missile (SAM) system in the Nile valley. In mid-April, Soviet pilots began flying a covering air patrol over the same region. Perhaps not without connection, the Soviet navy was engaging in what the daily newspaper of the Ministry of Defense called "the largest maneuvers in military history," executed simultaneously in the Pacific, Atlantic, Baltic, and Mediterranean.[3] In the late spring and early summer, the Soviets and the Egyptians attempted to move the line of air defense against Israeli attack up to the canal, but they were met by intensified Israeli counterstrikes that largely succeeded in frustrating their efforts. The military struggle in the early summer of 1970 was capped by the direct engagement of Soviet and Israeli air forces, in which the latter shot down four MIG-21s piloted by Soviet officers.

Earlier, Cairo and Jerusalem had accepted the American initiative for a cease-fire and a return to negotiations through the UN mediator, Gunnar Jarring. On the night the cease-fire went into effect, August 7–8, the Egyptians and the Soviets began to move the SAM line to the banks of the canal, in violation of the stand-still agreement, which formed an integral part of the cease-fire. For a while Washington pooh-poohed Jerusalem's protests, but even when the missile movements were confirmed by aerial photography, the State Department was unable to secure Egyptian and Soviet acknowledgment or "rectification" of the violations.

In September civil war broke out between the Fedayeen and Hussein's army in Jordan. Syrian armed forces crossed the Jordanian border, an action that threatened to trigger both Israeli and Great Power involvement. The Syrian intervention was turned back by the efforts of the Jordanian armed forces

[3] *Krasnaia zvezda,* 12 May, 1970.

themselves, and the danger of a renewal of Middle East war with Great Power involvement was averted, but not before Jerusalem and Washington had both uttered threatening noises. The same month brought the death of Nasser, the most powerful and charismatic figure that the Arab anti-Israel forces were able to muster.

Because of the violations of the stand-still agreement and in the absence of "rectification" of the SAM movements, Jerusalem refused to return to the Jarring negotiations. American efforts to compensate Israel for the deterioration in the tactical situation and to revive the Jarring talks brought about a significant reequipment and modernization of the Israel Defense Forces (IDF). But when, in February 1971, Jarring suggested that both sides undertake specific treaty commitments in advance of negotiations, including an Israeli pledge to withdraw from all Arab territories, Jerusalem refused and the Jarring talks broke down.

The most readily apparent result of the events of 1970 seemed to be a military stalemate between Egypt and Israel. Both sides welcomed the American initiative bringing about a cease-fire on the Suez Canal. In the year since Nasser had proclaimed the War of Attrition, the Israelis had sustained large and worrisome losses. Egyptian losses were considerably greater. Moreover, the campaign seemed to be heading for a dead end, for the Israeli air force was preventing the extension of the Egyptian SAM lines to the canal zone and therefore remained free to pound Egyptian artillery positions from the air.[4]

With the coming into effect of the cease-fire, the Israeli effort was nullified. Thus was established the most formidable air-defense system outside Eastern Europe and the USSR (not excluding North Vietnam), first in the Nile valley and around the Aswan Dam, then on the West Bank of the canal. The effort was intended in the first instance to deny the IDF the option of relatively low-cost counters to major Egyptian initiatives—for example, the aerial bombardment in response to the Egyptian army's concentrated artillery fire directed at the Bar-Lev line. Moving the missile line to the canal also unfurled an umbrella covering a good part of the East Bank to protect a future Egyptian crossing in force.

To some extent, the balance was redressed by the American reequipment of the IDF, which focused on electronics and airborne ground-attack systems. Moreover, under the cover of the cease-fire, the IDF was busy on its side of the canal as well, and undoubtedly the Bar-Lev line was made much less vulnerable

---

[4] According to Hassanein Heykal, Nasser accepted the cease-fire proposal because, among other reasons, "he had found out that the rate of military escalation on the Egyptian front required a pause to prepare for a new kind of war—electronic war" (*al-Ahram*, 3 December, 1970; citations from the Arab press and Soviet radio in this paper, unless otherwise indicated, are from Foreign Broadcast Information Service translations). Heykal discusses at length three other reasons for Nasser's decision—his desire for a political solution, his fear of the collapse of the "eastern front," and the psychological damage caused by the escalation of Soviet military involvement—but Heykal says nothing more about the need "to prepare for a new kind of war."

to sustained artillery barrages than it had been in 1969–1970. Prolongation of the cease-fire enabled both sides to further consolidate and improve their ground positions on either side of the Suez barrier.

The upshot seemed to be that the Egyptians would find the problem of a cross-canal attack more formidable than ever and the Israelis would face the difficult task of "solving" the canal's West Bank air-defense system. Presumably, because Cairo's subjective valuation of this balance of uncertainties was bleak, the cease-fire remained in *de facto* operation, even after President Sadat refused to renew it formally. To keep the cease-fire in force, the Israelis, for their part, indicated their willingness during 1971–1972 at least to discuss an interim agreement that required their withdrawal from the shelter of the Bar-Lev line.

But the balance of forces drawn in 1970 contained another major element whose effect only gradually became evident. The escalation of Soviet military involvement in the spring of 1970, culminating in the Soviet-Israeli dogfights over the canal, seemed to portend direct Soviet participation in any renewal of full-scale war between Israel and Egypt. The likelihood seemed particularly great if such a fourth round of Arab-Israeli war threatened another Egyptian and, therefore, also Soviet humiliation. The limits of the Soviet direct military engagement and the extent of possible American reaction became the burning issues of the day.[5]

On this critical question of the rules of the game of Soviet-American involvement in the Arab-Israeli conflict, the year 1970 brought some significant, but not immediately appreciated, lessons. At the beginning of the year, the Israeli deep-penetration raids threatened the collapse, not only of the Nasser-initiated War of Attrition, but also of the entire Egyptian war effort and perhaps of the regime itself. The USSR obviously had to come to the aid of its client in some way. A token response could have been useless in dangerous circumstances. A more effective response threatened to awaken U.S. fears and invite U.S. actions that would bring closer the danger that both superpowers had tried hard to avoid—their military confrontation in the region. In Moscow it might have been feared that the introduction of extensive Soviet forces on Egyptian soil could trigger exactly that kind of reaction. Thus, when it undertook to establish the air-defense system manned by its own forces in the Nile valley, the Kremlin was taking a step it very likely viewed as substantially risky. This should have applied *a fortiori* to the introduction of Soviet pilots flying MIG fighter patrols, but the American response to the first move had been weak. Moreover, Washington continued to withhold agreement to sell Israel more F-4s, hoping to secure Soviet cooperation in controlling arms supply to the region.

Encouraged by the American passivity in the face of the initial Soviet steps in

[5] In the spring of 1970, Israel's Minister of Defense Moshe Dayan gave the first subject considerable public attention. See his articles in *Maariv,* 10 April 1970, and in *Bamahaneh,* 14 April 1970.

February and March, Moscow felt emboldened to proceed to the second stage of sending Soviet pilots on combat air patrol in the Egyptian interior. Before the cease-fire came into effect, Soviet pilots ventured to engage Israeli fighters over the canal. Finally, confident in its estimate of Washington's reaction, the Kremlin dared to help break the standstill agreement and move the air-defense system to the edge of the canal.

In August 1970, Moscow might have been justified in drawing the conclusion that the American resolve to contain Soviet penetration had softened considerably over the years. Picture the response of an American policymaker a decade before to a Soviet attempt to introduce ten thousand military personnel into Egypt along with advanced jet fighters and SAMS, at the same time as a growing Soviet Mediterranean fleet was establishing a major quasi-base in Alexandria. If such a chain of events in 1970 failed to elicit a strong American response, perhaps it was ascribed in Moscow to the impact of the Vietnam experience. But it probably also appeared to the Kremlin that the graduated process of the growth of Soviet forces in the Middle East had played a major role in helping to alter Washington's perception of that growth. The cumulative results would surely have been unacceptable as a prospect ten years before—possibly even in the current period, had they taken place all at once. But perhaps the United States had not perceived the discrete turning points along the way toward the achievement of the end result. The policy of probing is, of course, a familiar feature of Soviet behavior in many parts of the world where the pursuit of Soviet interests encounters powerful opposition. The events of the first half of 1970 may have reinforced the view of Soviet decision makers on the value of incrementalism as a tactic of penetration in a contested area, given its seeming paralytic effect on U.S. policy.

However, the following month brought a moral of significantly different character. If paralysis of U.S. policy was attainable through a tactic of incremental introduction of Soviet forces, perhaps an important contributory factor was Washington's appreciation of the size of the Soviet investment in Egypt, the significance of the Soviet position there to Moscow's entire policy in the region, and the threat contained in the IDF's deep-penetration raids. Only in these circumstances, it might be argued, was U.S. disposition to act lessened. When the balance of interests was reversed, Moscow was put on notice that the old tiger still had some teeth. In September, Syrian intervention in the Jordanian civil war brought the U.S. Sixth Fleet back into the Eastern Mediterranean. The Nixon Administration gave evidence of its readiness to join with Israel in preventing a takeover in Jordan by the Soviet-supplied and-aided Syrian forces. Soviet reaction to this episode will be examined in more detail below, but it can be summarized here as an effort to appear to have had an important hand in the outcome while behaving with circumspection. In a situation where American traditional interests were endangered and where the Kremlin saw only secondary interests of its own involved, Washington's willingness to adopt a forceful position encountered only a muted response from Moscow.

Thus, the experience of the first semester of 1970 demonstrated the Soviet commitment to defend the heartland of Egypt, to prevent the collapse of the pillar of Soviet policy in the Middle East. It also demonstrated that Washington was not prepared to interfere with the Kremlin in this sphere. But the second half of 1970 brought a concrete demonstration of U.S. readiness to defend its important regional interests. Moscow had reason to suspect that a Soviet-sponsored invasion of the Sinai would be received entirely differently by the Americans, who stressed the unacceptability of Soviet participation in an effort that might quickly be transformed into a challenge to Israel's existence within the pre-1967 lines.

These elements of the local military balance—the apparent military stalemate consequent on the cease-fire and the delimitation of the bounds of Soviet engagement—exerted increasing pressure on the Egyptian-Soviet alliance. Discouraged by the costliness of the War of Attrition, fearful that the cross-canal invasion was beyond their unaided capabilities, the Egyptians sought a guarantee of success in an attempt to expel the IDF from the Sinai. This was the conundrum that led to the dramatic exodus of Soviet military personnel in July 1972.

Cairo publicly protested the Kremlin's refusal to supply "offensive" arms, and this refusal was blamed for the postponement of the "inevitable" battle with Israel.[6] President Sadat demanded surface-to-surface missiles and MIG-25s, but his insistence on the criticality of particular weapons systems put the cart before the horse. The Egyptian army had the wherewithal for a cross-canal push, but it sought a *guarantee* of success against its formidable opponent. This could be attained not by means of particular weapons systems but only through the commitment of substantial Soviet forces in attack.[7] That the Russians were unwilling to do anything of the sort was long suspected but had not yet been accepted in 1970.[8] Having finally to face up to that bitter fact, Sadat expelled his benefactors. "The Russians had become a burden to us. They would not fight

---

[6] Lack of "offensive" weapons hindered him in other aspects of the conflict with Israel, Sadat claimed: "If I had a fighter-bomber, I would not have allowed Israel to commit its aggression in southern Lebanon as it has done recently." Quoted by Selim Louzi, editor of the Beirut weekly, *al-Hawadess,* as cited in the *Jerusalem Post,* 6 October 1972.

[7] A guarantee of success required Soviet troop commitments, not only because of uncertainty about the combat effectiveness of the Egyptian army, but also because of the nature of the weapons systems demanded. Whether the MIG-25 is as effective in combat as it is in high-altitude, high-speed reconnaissance remains to be demonstrated. Surface-to-surface missiles with high-explosive warheads are notoriously inaccurate. If they were to be used as "city-busters," and especially if they were armed with nuclear warheads, they would invite Israeli preemption or American intervention. If Moscow was prepared to supply the missiles for such a mission, it would have had to be prepared for massive commitment of its own forces.

[8] See text pp. 99–101.

and would give our enemy an excuse for seeking American support and assistance."[9] Thus, in its fragile progression, the cease-fire of 1970 seemed to have tipped the military balance to the Israeli side.[10] The Russians "would not fight," and without their weight applied massively and directly, the defense seemed to have the upper hand in the canal exchange.

The Egyptian-Soviet rift in 1972 underscored the significance of another major event of 1970. The death of Nasser on September 28, removed from the scene the Arab leader who had been the mainstay of Soviet policy in the Middle East. It is true that in 1967 Nasser had brought his Soviet friends to the edge of disaster, but the blame had to be shared by Moscow, which had at least led him astray. Nasser's swift reestablishment of his authority, with the help of the Cairo street demonstrations of June 9–10, also insured the preservation of Soviet influence in Egypt. Mollified by the hasty rearmament of Egypt and Syria and by vigorous international political support of the Arab cause, Nasser forgave the Russians their failure to come to his aid at the beginning of June. In turn, the Kremlin saw Nasser as the dynamic figure who could purge the armed forces of dissident elements, radicalize the society, and cooperate militarily and politically with Moscow. The Soviet leadership was surely sincere in its cable of condolence to the Egyptians mourning Nasser as "a great friend of the Soviet Union," as a "tested and consistent fighter against imperialism," as the man responsible for the fact that "the UAR held a vanguard position in the national liberation movement of the Arab peoples."[11]

Sadat, for all his recent achievements, has not earned the Kremlin's admiration. Any Egyptian figure coming after Nasser would most likely have been a less forceful and colorful personality. But Nasser's departure from the scene meant more than just the loss of a dynamic and personable leader of the pro-Soviet camp. His replacement was actively involved in a rapid deterioration of Soviet-Egyptian relations. Barely eight months after his entrance into office, Sadat purged the Ali Sabri faction and had its members sentenced to long prison terms. When Podgorny was hastily dispatched to Cairo to repair the damage, he secured Sadat's signature on a Treaty of Friendship that called for prior Egyptian consultation with Moscow on major policy issues. But Sadat's signature did not hinder him from helping Numeiry in Sudan quash a Communist-led coup in July 1971, nor from setting deadlines for the resumption of hostilities against Israel without consulting the power that was supposed to rescue him from the consequences of his saber-rattling. Most important of all, of course, Sadat demonstrated the real value of the treaty by expelling the Russian presence in July 1972.

[9] Louzi, *Jerusalem Post,* 6 October 1972.
[10] For a typical view of Israel's prewar military position, see Ronald M. DeVore, "The Arab-Israeli Military Balance," *Military Review,* (Nov. 1973) 65–71, reprinted from *Revue Militaire Générale* (March 1973).
[11] *Izvestiia,* 30 September 1970.

Not entirely without connection, Moscow began to put more emphasis on its Iraqi and Syrian connections. A Treaty of Friendship was concluded with Baghdad, several high-level delegations were exchanged, and the Soviet press was clamorous in its support of the June 1, 1972, nationalization of Iraq Petroleum Company properties. Special marks of favor were shown Syria, including the unprecedented announcement of a shipment of arms. Whether Syria or Iraq could, without significant loss, replace Egypt as the linchpin of the Soviet Union's Middle East policy is debatable, but that is not of direct concern here. The point is that Sadat was not Nasser and the Soviet maneuverings reflected that significant fact.

No doubt, in the wake of the October 1973 war and the oil embargo, the Kremlin takes a kindlier view of Sadat. The impact of the October war is discussed at a later point, but with respect to Sadat, it can be said here that his dependence on King Faisal and the possibility of rapprochement with the United States must be viewed with some concern in Moscow. The importance of Soviet-supplied arms notwithstanding, Sadat has not been a reliable ally and there seems little reason why the Kremlin should expect substantial change in this regard.[12]

September 1970 also marked a profound reversal in the fortunes of the Palestinian Fedayeen. Their defeat at the hands of King Hussein's army erased a major threat to the viability of his rule in Jordan. Hashemite Jordan was reestablished as a factor independent of radical Arab forces and thus as one on which American policy could place some reliance. The defeat of the Fedayeen also meant the postponement of Egyptian hopes for the creation of an "eastern front" (Syria and Jordan) and paralyzed a radicalizing influence in inter-Arab politics. These developments signified a reverse for the USSR as well.

It may be that the Kremlin committed a significant error in regarding the Jordanian civil war as involving only tangential Soviet interests. Perhaps Moscow did not view the actual outcome as final; indeed, the expulsion of the Fedayeen from Jordan was not finally achieved until the following year. Nevertheless, the defeat of the Fedayeen can be viewed as an important setback to the USSR because it helped prevent the polarization of forces in the Middle East.

Polarization constituted one of the two major nightmares of U.S. policy, the other being, of course, superpower military confrontation. All along, Washington had sought to prevent the alignment of the Arab states on the side of the USSR, leaving the United States alone with Israel in the region. To forestall polarization, Washington had to obtain the neutrality, if not the loyalty, of at least some Arab states, but it also had to prevent the broadening of the front of Arab-Israel conflict. Since this was the one issue on which Arab states had to provide at least

[12] The Soviets had their troubles with Nasser too. But the stormy period in their relationship came earlier, during the period of the Syrian-Egyptian union and the competition between Nasser and Kassem of Iraq (1958–1961). By 1964, Khrushchev was awarding Nasser the highest honors as a Hero of the Soviet Union.

protestations of Arab unity, the broadening of the Arab-Israeli conflict risked intensifying anti-American manifestations; it might lead to such radicalization as to completely erode the U.S. position. This set of events was one of the major dangers foreseen in the conflict between the Fedayeen and Israel. Israeli reprisals on Jordanian and Lebanese territory were viewed with alarm in Washington as running the danger of throwing these countries, too, into the radical Arab camp. Thus, the destruction of the Fedayeen position in Jordan was a significant factor in averting the dangers Washington had foreseen.[13]

The history of Soviet relations with the Fedayeen remains to be written. Nonetheless, it is apparent that before the September 1970 events Moscow had begun to take a closer look at the Palestinian movements, and Soviet rhetoric on this topic had undergone some subtle changes. In the year before the Six-Day War, Moscow took a curiously passive attitude to Syrian-backed Fatah incursions into Israel. To Israeli remonstrances, the Soviets responded that terrorists were figments of Israeli propaganda or else they denied the seriousness of the situation. Perhaps in belated recognition of the provocative role of the Fatah, the Soviet attitude to the Fedayeen after the June War was patently hostile. As late as the summer of 1968, the pro-Soviet Arab Communist parties denounced the "romantic and reckless course advocated by progressive national patriotic elements of the petty bourgeoisie, horrified by military defeat."[14] Even in the following spring, a Soviet writer termed the goal of "liquidation of the State of Israel and the creation of a 'Palestinian democratic state' . . . not realistic." He opposed the notion that "the problem of Palestinian refugees should be accorded first priority in a Middle Eastern political settlement," on the grounds that this would "complicate the solution of the task of liquidating the consequences of the 1967 Israeli aggression and also, in the end, the solution of the Palestinian problem."[15]

In the last half of 1969 there were signs of reappraisal: attacks on the Fedayeen ceased, their cross-border attacks were explicitly and more frequently praised, and, on November 27, the Central Committee of the Warsaw Pact countries (Romania abstaining) for the first time raised the issue of "the legitimate right and interests of the Arab people of Palestine."[16] At the beginning of 1970, Arafat was invited to Moscow, although on an unofficial

[13] King Hussein's successful campaign against the Fedayeen did not completely liquidate their provocative role in the Arab-Israeli conflict. Their presence in some force in Lebanon and Syria resulted in occasional flare-ups during 1971–1972 along the borders of these countries with Israel. However, the withdrawal of Jordan from the coalition of sanctuary-hosts crippled Fedayeen effectiveness. It tended to encourage resistance by the Lebanese government to the freewheeling Fedayeen activities and, therefore, also to eliminate one basis of American pressure on Israel.

[14] An-Nida (Beirut), 4 July 1968.

[15] G. Dad'iants, in Sovetskaia Rossiia, 15 April 1969. Dad'iants was a "political observer" of the Novosti News Agency.

[16] TASS, 27 November 1969.

basis. Evidently, these developments reflected a Soviet decision that Moscow could not stand aside from an attempt to influence what appeared increasingly to be one of the most important political developments in the Middle East.

Whatever defensive strands may be identified in the Soviet motivation to develop closer relations with the Fedayeen (e.g., fear of large-scale war triggered by their attacks on Israel), it is also necessary to allow for Moscow's desire to maintain and expand its influence in the region. Both aspects may have had an important Chinese dimension. Ties between the Fedayeen and Peking predated the Six-Day War, and the USSR had previously displayed its sensitivity to Chinese Communist competition in the Middle East. With respect to Sino-Fedayeen ties, the issue was not so much arms supply as ideological-political orientation. Concerned about its leadership in the Communist world, Moscow was loath to see Peking establish a foothold in the region of greatest Soviet investment. The USSR was presumably also anxious not to be dragged into conflict with the United States by forces over which it had no control.[17]

The Soviet approach to the Fedayeen had to be cautious, given the evident inconsistency of full support of the Fedayeen with the line of "political solution," whose foundation is the November 1967 Security Council resolution. Among the few things that are clear in that resolution is that the State of Israel is seen as a party to the settlement. On the other hand, the Fedayeen called for liquidation of the State of Israel.

It is not self-evident that the Fedayeen reaction to Soviet rapprochment would have been necessarily enthusiastic. True, they would not have been overconcerned about Western reactions, given the existing hostility to the United States and Britain. Perhaps there would have been a receptivity to Soviet overtures inherent in the radical rhetoric of the movement. However, it is doubtful that the Popular Front, the major Fedayeen faction with an articulated radical ideology, was anxious to see itself swallowed in a Moscow embrace. Fatah, the largest organization in the group, would certainly have been jealous of its freedom of action and possibly wary of splitting the movement by too close identification with Moscow. Perhaps it was in part for these reasons that the Arab Communist parties chose to organize their own Fedayeen organization, al-Ansar, early in 1970, rather than operate through any of the existing ones. The Soviets might have had to hold out a very large carrot to obtain a significant voice in Fedayeen affairs.

In any case, if the Soviets had a Fedayeen card, its play was preempted by the September 1970 events. Thereafter, Moscow continued to try to keep communication lines open to the Fedayeen, maintaining friendly but unofficial relations

[17]Given its own muted and cautious reaction to the Jordanian civil war, the Kremlin was visibly irked by the freewheeling propaganda emanating from Peking. "Anyone of sound mind," Radio Moscow lectured the Chinese on October 9, 1970, would recognize that a civil war was "against the interests of the Arab people and the Palestinian revolution. But Chinese representatives instigated the Palestinians to provoke such a conflict."

with Fatah, the largest and least radical component of the movement. But the weaknesses of the Fedayeen were still too great to make partnership an immediately realizable option.

The Kremlin now seems to be taking the initiative in seeking to create a role for the Palestinians at the Geneva peace conference, presumably on the basis of abandonment of the objective of liquidating the State of Israel. A Soviet note to the Palestine Liberation Organization (PLO) prodded the Fedayeen umbrella organization to reconsider its views on the creation of a Palestinian state, and Soviet leaders have insisted in private talks with Western counterparts that the Fedayeen movement would have to be represented at a Middle East peace conference.[18]

Perhaps this reflects Soviet annoyance at the dominant role of the Americans in the ending of the October war and the planning of the peace conference. But given Hussein's aspirations to recover the West Bank, if only in loose confederational relation to the East Bank, and Israel's deeply rooted conviction of the inevitable irredentism of a Palestinian entity on the West Bank, especially one ruled by Fatah, a major role for the PLO at the peace conference is hardly a foregone conclusion.

However, if the PLO does take a participant's seat at the peace table, it will have acknowledged its readiness to recognize Israel's right to independent existence, at least on the formal level. Such a major policy change, if it occurs, would reflect the recognition that the movement was too weak to continue to insist on its maximal objectives. If it cannot manage the transformation without tearing itself apart, the Fedayeen movement will face the threat, as Trotsky would have put it, of "being cast into the dustbin of history." In either case, September 1970 was clearly the turning point.

III. Soviet-American Military Interactions in the Middle East

In the summer of 1970, Soviet-piloted MIG-21s engaged Israeli fighters in aerial combat over the banks of the Suez Canal. This was the culmination of a deployment of Soviet military forces in the Middle East that constituted the most conspicuous and probably also the most significant change in the regional environment during the 1960s. Most of the Soviet force left Egyptian soil after the break in July 1972. Nevertheless, on the outbreak of war in October 1973, Moscow sharply increased the strength of its Mediterranean fleet, airlifted vast quantities of arms to Egypt and Syria, and threatened to intervene to save an Egyptian army from being throttled in an Israeli encirclement. In the meantime, the rapid buildup of its strategic nuclear forces after Khrushchev's dismissal brought the Soviet Union a position of formally acknowledged "parity" with the United States in the global balance. Under these dramatic shifts in regional and global power relations, how are the rules of the superpower military game being

[18] *The New York Times*, 1, 2, and 21 November 1973.

fixed in the Middle East? Has the likelihood of an armed clash between Soviet and American forces in the region increased? Under what conditions is military confrontation possible?

To begin with, it seems unlikely that the strategic rivalry between the United States and the USSR will in the foreseeable future again become a major focus of either nation's policy in the Middle East. Technology can never be fully predicted, but there seems to be nothing on the technological horizon that is likely to recreate the situation of the 1950s.[19] U.S. forces in the Middle East still have general war capabilities, embodied in the nuclear-tipped missiles of Polaris-Poseidon submarines plying the Mediterranean, as well as in the nuclear payload of the Sixth Fleet's carrier aircraft. Since 1967 the Soviet regional forces designed to counter this strategic threat have been significantly strengthened. Missile-cruisers, submarines, and helicopter carriers[20] appearing in force have undoubtedly taken the edge off the Sixth Fleet's power.

A threat to the survivability of the Sixth Fleet is also posed by Soviet or radical Arab aircraft based on the southern littoral of the sea, although the threat is potential rather than actual. The number of usable jet aircraft bases in North Africa is large, and should Soviet forces appear west of Egypt as they have there, the danger to the Sixth Fleet would become significant and concrete.

But these considerations do not affect the central point. Whereas in the era of the relatively short-legged B-47 the Middle East was believed to have strategic importance for the superpower contest, in the third or fourth generation of ICBMs the strategic balance will continue to operate as a constraint on Soviet and American policy in the Middle East but hardly as the focus of a struggle for control over the region.

On the strategic question itself, there is no gainsaying that, as Brzezinski has put it, "The central reality of the American-Soviet power relationship . . . is mutual non-survivability in the event of comprehensive war."[21] But this is not intended as the guide to the future behavior of the superpowers. Indeed, there is no rational alternative to the pursuit of mutual accommodation when the world is threatened by nuclear annihilation, as leaders on both sides frequently declare. Yet the pursuit of accommodation does not exhaustively describe Soviet-American relations in any arena of their competition, certainly not in third areas. Clearly, neither government is likely to attempt to destroy the other's forces in one particular region of the world in order to alter the global strategic balance. The balance of nuclear power depends upon forces located elsewhere, which are invulnerable to actions taken in the Middle East itself. No conceivable

[19] This point was made in an unpublished paper by Arnold Horelick.
[20] Presumably to be joined soon by the USSR's first fixed-wing aircraft carrier now being readied in the Black Sea.
[21] Zbigniew Brzezinski, "U.S.A./USSR: The Power Relationship," cited in *International Negotiation. The Impact of the Changing Power Balance*, compiled by the Subcommittee on National Security and International Operations of the Committee on Government Operations of the U.S. Senate (Washington, D.C.: U.S. Gov't. Printing Office, 1971), p. 8.

strategic rationale would justify an attempt to eliminate the adversary's forces in the region.

The possibility of confrontation through accident is often mentioned. The fleets of the United States and the USSR in the Mediterranean have over a number of years engaged in sophisticated games of "chicken," in which near-brushes have been frequent. There are also possibilities of incidents in which the action of one of the superpowers may be misread as preparation for deliberate attack on the local forces of the other. The outstanding case in point is the dispatch of units of the Sixth Fleet to the scene of the Israeli attack on the U.S.S. *Liberty,* an American intelligence-monitoring ship, in the last phase of the Six-Day War. Dealing with such problems of accidental war can be negotiated by treaty, as in the Moscow summit arrangement of May 1972, to define the "rules of the road" at sea. Over the years there have developed tacit agreements between the forces of both sides that have regulated the interaction in order to defuse such incidents. At the time of the *Liberty* affair, President Johnson hastened to use the Hot Line to avoid arousing Soviet fears about a fleet maneuver that might have seemed threatening.

The major danger of superpower confrontation is posed by the risk of involvement through the clash of their local interests. Here we find one of the more common generalizations about Soviet-American interaction. It has been said that strategic inferiority stayed the Soviet hand in earlier crises, such as those of Cuba and Berlin, but as the USSR approached a position of strategic parity with the United States, Soviet behavior in third areas might be expected to become more audacious. Washington responses might then be expected to become more circumspect as the global balance turned less favorable. Hurewitz noted that "the novelty in the Arab-Israeli third round [i.e., June 1967] was not the Kremlin's signal to the White House that the Soviet Union would not intervene, but the American counter signal that the United States also would not."[22] Of course, the Israelis secured the upper hand immediately and the United States did not have to intervene, although it is possible that the situation was not yet clear to Washington at that point. Nevertheless, the White House hastened to make clear to the Kremlin that Soviet forbearance would be matched on the part of U.S. forces. Apparently, the administration was delighted to be able to avoid a situation in which the possibility of confronting Soviet power might arise at all. Considering that the Sixth Fleet's superiority over the Soviet Mediterranean Squadron was unquestioned at the time, it appears that Washington was apprehensive over the possible "tripwire" role that Soviet Mediterranean forces might play. The mere presence of a Soviet force exerted an inhibiting effect upon Washington's freedom of action. It has there-

---

[22] J. C. Hurewitz, "Changing Military Perspectives in the Middle East," in P. Y. Hammond and S. S. Alexander, eds., *Political Dynamics in the Middle East* (New York: American Elsevier, 1972), p. 72.

fore been frequently asserted, even by those who have taken a jaundiced view of Soviet prospects in the region, that a repetition of the United States operation in Lebanon in 1958 was no longer possible in the Middle East.[23]

However, as Goldhamer has argued, the postulate of a direct relation between the Kremlin's aggressiveness and the favorableness of the strategic balance is at best an oversimplification, if not actually a misreading of the historical record.[24] Soviet policy has experienced twists and turns, but these are difficult to relate to changes in the strategic outlook. Moscow's stance in the early years after World War II was aggressive and activist when its strategic inferiority was greatest; its political line in the third world "softened" in the middle 1950s when the American nuclear lead was being whittled down. In fact, "postwar negative correlation between Soviet aggressiveness and improvement in her strategic position may be a causal relation—that is, inferiority and its perception produce an aggressive reaction to ward off the dangers of weakness."[25] Aggressive behavior *may* appear under conditions of growing strength, as was the case with Soviet policy in the Middle East in the mid-1960s, which suggests that knowledge of context and circumstances is crucial to understanding of the process. If the notion of balance encompasses more than just the relative size of intercontinental nuclear forces but also that of conventional forces, the general political atmosphere, and the comparative morale of both sides' diplomacy, Goldhamer indicates, the direct relationship between increasing power and increasing aggressiveness may be a better fit of the facts.

The introduction of the elements of political environment and perceived determination of one side or the other complicates the equation but points to a more realistic approach. Thus, the outcome of a crisis of political confrontation between the superpowers may be said to depend on the establishment of relative credibility. Brzezinski has said that where mutual nonsurvivability is assured, the credibility of either side is achieved by will alone, which tempts both protagonists to elaborate bluff.[26] Presumably, power A must perceive and be overawed by the intensity of power B's will to achieve the particular goal. Only if A can be convinced that the goal is so important to B that the latter is prepared to risk all can B's credibility be established. Thus, A's perception of the overall priority B accords his goal, rather than relative strategic superiority per se, ultimately determines which protagonist prevails in a crisis.[27] One must add, following Goldhamer, the general political environment and the perception of each other's

---

[23] Paradoxically, the same school of thought also holds that in a showdown, the Soviet Squadron would be no match for the Sixth Fleet.

[24] Herbert Goldhamer, *The Soviet Union in a Period of Strategic Parity,* R-889 (Santa Monica, Calif.: The Rand Corporation, November 1971).

[25] *Ibid.,* p. 33.

[26] Brzezinski, "U.S.A./USSR," p. 11.

[27] See also Alexander L. George, Daniel K. Hall, and William R. Simon, *The Limits of Coercive Diplomacy: Laos, Cuba, Vietnam* (Boston: Little, Brown, 1971).

political strengths and weaknesses as factors in establishing the credibility of each side's political-military posture.

This relates to situations in which the threat of central war is a tangible factor influencing both sides' calculations. Are there military actions the USSR can undertake against U.S. or NATO forces in the Middle East that would not involve a high probability of general war? Gasteyger has argued that the Soviet presence in the Mediterranean would "make it easy for her to cut important supply lines to Europe during a crisis. If one remembers that in any one day there are usually about 2,600 merchant ships in the Mediterranean . . . one can appreciate the degree of Western vulnerability to any threat coming from a powerful adversary."[28] Evidently, Gasteyger foresaw the possibility of the USSR's undertaking blockade or interdiction of the sea-lanes leading to the northern shores of the Mediterranean. However, he did not explicitly address the question of how the USSR could expect to interfere with Western sea or air communications and still keep the conflict in the framework of a limited war.

The threat postulated by Gasteyger belongs to the general category known as "outflanking NATO from the south."[29] Soviet submarine-launched ballistic missiles (SLBMs) in the Mediterranean may enhance the military threat to NATO's southern flank over and above the land-based nuclear forces targeted thereon, although many observers believe that the Soviet Squadron has serious weaknesses in a nuclear offensive role, even granting the degradation of the Sixth Fleet's power. If the NATO alliance were interpreted unambiguously to mean that a threat to one member was a threat to all, it is difficult to see why a threat from the south would more likely be confronted only with limited power than a threat from the north. A Soviet attack on Greece from naval units in the Mediterranean—provided, again, that the alliance held up—would be indistinguishable from an attack by ground forces along any of the ground fronts in Europe.

A less common formulation of the outflanking threat is the possibility of proxy threats to NATO members—for example, by Bulgaria. The major problem with scenarios of this type is that Moscow might find it hard to believe that an attack on Greece or Turkey by a Bulgarian army would not imply a very high probability of U.S. involvement. If the use of a proxy is to significantly diminish the likelihood of triggering a NATO response, the result would be conditional on increasing disaffection between NATO's western and eastern wings or an apparent U.S. reluctance to walk the brink over Greece or Turkey.

This suggests, in fact, that the threat to NATO resides not in a classic military outflanking maneuver but in the more subtle danger of the dissolution of alliance ties, of the rupture of solidarity between its southern and western flanks

[28] Curt Gasteyger, *Conflict and Tension in the Mediterranean,* Adelphi Papers, number 51 (London: The Institute for Strategic Studies, Sept. 1968), p. 5.
[29] Gasteyger, however, insists that cutting supply lines is different from "outflanking."

on the one hand, or with the United States on the other. How much Soviet power in the Mediterranean, or the Soviet Squadron specifically, contributes to this danger is not easy to appraise. However, there is a strong desire in Europe to bury the cold war. American response to the growth of Soviet forces in the Mediterranean seems to many to pose a danger of nuclear war. The U.S. effort to resupply Israel via European staging areas to counter the Soviet airlift during the October War and the subsequent worldwide alert of U.S. forces, called when the Kremlin seemed to be contemplating direct intervention, were met by resentment and official disassociation in Western Europe.

In general, however, the idea that the buildup of Soviet military presence in the Mediterranean has limited U.S. freedom to exert power in the region relates not so much to the problem of outflanking NATO as to that of the application of U.S. power on the southern and eastern littorals of the Mediterranean. Even if it wished to, Washington could not often engage in gunboat diplomacy in the Middle East because the environment of radical nationalism makes that an outmoded form of international "discourse." But to what extent is the Russian presence a significant contributing deterrent, owing to U.S. fear that the superpowers will clash through a process of escalation in defense of their local interests? The willingness of the powers to confront one another may depend in part on their estimate of the likelihood of victory based on the local military balance, but, more important, it will hinge on their perception of the extent of each side's "vital interests" in the region, on considerations of the other power's determination to resist, and on the degree of confidence either may have that local conflict will not get out of hand and escalate uncontrollably to general war.

Suppose a government of Lebanon, "duly constituted and recognized," were to seek U.S. aid to prevent a Syrian-supported Fedayeen takeover. On finding ships of the Sixth Fleet steaming toward Beirut, would elements of the Soviet Mediterranean Squadron interpose themselves between the American ships and the Lebanese shore? Would the Soviet ships fire on the incoming American forces? If the Sixth Fleet's superiority is manifest, would Moscow be ready to confront American power in a situation that might bring on a humiliating defeat in a limited war or require the threat of nuclear war to provide a good chance of a favorable outcome?

An analogous dilemma presented itself to Soviet decision makers in September 1970, in connection with the Jordanian-Syrian crisis. In barest outline, the events in Jordan may be summarized as follows[30] : As the culmination of months of intermittent clashes between the Jordanian Army and Fedayeen forces, and after the hijacking of three airliners that were then forced to land in a Fedayeen-controlled field in northern Jordan, full-scale fighting broke out on

---

[30] For additional detail on the course of the crisis and on U.S. policy, see Henry Brandon's part ("Were We Masterful . . . ") of the dialogue on "Jordan: The Forgotten Crisis," *Foreign Policy* (Spring 1973): 158–70.

September 17. Hussein's troops were in control of the south, but the battle raged on in Amman while the Fedayeen held large parts of the north. On September 19, Amman accused Damascus of an invasion of Jordan with armored forces; two armored columns crossed the frontier from Syria early on the twentieth. Initially, a Jordanian attempt to throw back the Syrian column fared badly, and the King was alarmed enough to ask the United States and Britain to consider what military aid could be quickly supplied to him. On the twenty-second, Jordanian Hawker Hunters attacked the Syrian tanks, inflicting considerable damage, and the Syrians began to withdraw the following day.

From the inception of the crisis, the possibility of American intervention loomed large. On September 17, the Chicago *Sun Times* quoted President Nixon as saying that the United States might intervene if Syria or Iraq intervened. The President also hinted that the Soviets should not count on Washington's "rationality" or predictability. On the nineteenth, Secretary Rogers denounced the Syrian invasion and declared that it threatened to widen the war. Administration hints of possible intervention were transmitted in a variety of inspired leaks. With reinforcements from the Atlantic on the way, the Sixth Fleet was dispatched to patrol off the coasts of Israel and Lebanon; American troops were alerted in both the United States and Europe. Simultaneously, Moscow was being warned directly of the dangers inherent in the Syrian action. Moreover, the Israelis had mobilized partially, moving 400 tanks to the Golan Heights and putting their air force on alert. A U.S.-backed Israeli intervention loomed as a serious possibility.

How did the Soviets respond? Private representations to Washington stressed the Kremlin's efforts to prevent a widening of the war.[31] Publicly, Moscow confined itself to deploring the fratricidal conflict in Jordan and to pointing out the opportunity being offered for imperialist intervention. On September 20, the first official and public Soviet reaction came in the form of a statement by the state news agency. The statement expressed "alarm" at reports of the Sixth Fleet movements to the eastern Mediterranean and of plans for foreign military intervention. "Such development of events would aggravate the situation in the Middle East and . . . would essentially complicate the international situation as such. The situation in Jordan and around it causes deep concern in the Soviet Union. . . ." The final two paragraphs are worth citing in full:

> It is believed in the Soviet Union that foreign armed intervention in the events in Jordan would aggravate the conflict, hamper the Arab nations' struggle for liquidating the consequences of Israel's aggression, for a lasting peace with justice in the Middle East, for restoration of their violated rights and national interests. All who cherish the cause of peace and come out for strengthening international security cannot put up with such a development.
>
> The Arab countries and peoples may be confident that the Soviet Union will

[31] *Ibid.*

continue to pursue a policy of supporting their just struggle for ensuring their full independence and national development, for preserving and strengthening the peace of the world.[32]

The following day, September 21, a Radio Moscow broadcast in Arabic seemed to promise only sympathy: "Should the U.S. military intervention in Jordan take place, it would further aggravate the Middle East crisis and make the Arab struggle to remove the consequences of Israeli aggression and to regain their usurped rights and national interests more difficult." By the evening of September 21, the Kremlin was hinting that it was cautioning the Syrians while simultaneously urging Washington to restrain the Israelis from moving in on the battle. According to *The New York Times'* account of October 8, ships of the Soviet Squadron kept close tabs on the Sixth Fleet during the crisis, even intermingling with American warships. After the immediate crisis passed, the Soviets staged a show of force,[33] but no effort was made at any time to interfere with Sixth Fleet movements. Moscow was careful to provide no signal that it contemplated frustrating American designs by force.

After the crisis peak, too, Brezhnev felt it possible at Baku on October 2 to warn that "one may not only burn one's fingers but may even lose one's hand."[34] But the sentence immediately following spoke of the "stormy reaction" and "demonstration of the *peoples'* wrath" (emphasis supplied) that would have been triggered by "imperialist military intervention."[35]

---

[32] TASS, 20 September 1970.

[33] Between the twenty-seventh of September and the twenty-seventh of November four Soviet cruisers, fourteen destroyers, five submarines, and various other vessels passed into the Mediterranean from the Black Sea. During the same period, two cruisers, six destroyers, two submarines, and various other support vessels left the Mediterranean to return to the Black Sea. There was therefore a net increase in the Mediterranean Squadron of two cruisers, eight destroyers, three submarines, and a patrol vessel. The number of support ships was drawn down in various categories. *Cumhuriyet* (Istanbul), 7 December 1970.

[34] *Pravda,* 3 October 1970. The echo of Khrushchev's missile-rattling in November 1956, *after* becoming convinced that the United States would not intervene on the Anglo-French-Israeli side, is weak but still striking.

[35] In the second half of the dialogue on "Jordan: The Forgotten Crisis," cited in Note 30, David Schoenbaum ("Or Lucky," pp. 171–181) concludes that the United States "was very lucky in September 1970" (p. 181), because the threats to intervene were not credible. Schoenbaum's case rests on evidence of inadequacy of the military means, the lack of suitable friendly bases in the Middle East, and post-Cambodia domestic opposition to U.S. involvement in another war. He suggests that only the Israeli threat to intervene was credible to Syrians and Russians alike.

  Schoenbaum's argument is unconvincing because it ignores the actual Soviet response. Had Moscow perceived the U.S. moves as empty bluff, the Soviet reaction would hardly have been as restrained as it was in fact. The threat of an IDF intervention should have occasioned a vigorous attempt to head it off—in the manner of the propaganda campaigns of 1966–1967. It was the credible threat of U.S. backing for Israeli intervention that made the Kremlin circumspect. Schoenbaum himself admits "there are plausible reasons" for believing the American threat was credible in at least some respects: "All international politics has an element of psychodrama. Great Powers, including the United States, live by their capacity to inspire confidence in some, uncertainty in others" (p. 179).

The Soviet media portrayed the USSR as having had an important role in damping down the crisis and in preventing U.S. intervention. A *Pravda* review by Vitaly Korionov declared:

The decisive rebuff which met Washington's attempt to heat up the situation in the Middle East region is sufficiently instructive. According to the unanimous appraisal of the international public, the Soviet Union's firm, consistent, peace-loving policy was of special importance in sobering the "hotheads" in the Pentagon. In their turn, the Arab government leaders—and the late Gamal Abdel Nasser played a particularly important role in this—found it within their power to normalize the situation in Jordan.[36]

Krasnaia zvezda of the same date went even further, claiming that the "Jordanian events reaffirmed that the Arab countries, which are striving for a political settlement of the Middle East conflict, can count on the Soviet Union's support in the future, too." Thus, the Soviet Union made the retrospective claim that far from having acted circumspectly, it was instrumental in organizing collective action of the Arab states to help stop the fratricide before U.S. forces could intervene.[37]

What would have happened if the superpower roles had been reversed, if, say, Soviet forces had been dispatched to put down a counterrevolution against a Moscow-oriented Syrian regime? Lewis has argued that a "Lebanon-1958" type of operation could not be carried out now by the Russians either, for the same "tripwire" reasons alleged to impede U.S. action.[38] The Soviet Mediterranean Squadron is considered weak in important respects—organic air defense, amphibious attack, and ground support. A moderate-sized, sophisticated air force could constitute a serious threat to the Squadron. However, what appears to be a significant weakness in theory may not be so in fact. If attacked by the Soviets, the Israelis might well respond in kind. But short of a Soviet first strike on the Sixth Fleet, would the latter be likely to be put into action against the Soviet Squadron if the Soviets were mounting a "Lebanon 1958" operation of their own?

The resolution of such crises probably depends more on the balance of perceived interests than on that of arms. Given the strong uncertainties as to the outcome of a superpower engagement, even with conventional weaponry, neither power will want to risk a military clash, other things being equal, except in defense of a major interest that the other side can be counted on to recognize. In face of American power mobilizing to protect a U.S. client in Jordan, the USSR

---

[36] *Pravda,* 4 October 1970.
[37] See also D. Volsky, "Lessons of the Jordan Crisis," *New Times,* (no. 42, October 21, 1970): 8; and a statement by the Lebanese Communist Party Central Committee in *an-Nida* (Beirut), 24 October 1970.
[38] Bernard Lewis, "The Great Powers, the Arabs and the Israelis," *Foreign Affairs* 47, no. 4 (July 1969):644.

saw no compelling reason to risk war with the United States. If the retreat of the
Syrian tanks had been followed by an Israeli armored thrust against Damascus,
Moscow might have bared its teeth, as it threatened to do on Saturday, June 10,
1967. The same logic would hold for a Soviet-mounted "Lebanon 1958"
operation: It is unlikely that the United States would feel compelled to threaten
intervention unless an invasion of Jordan, Israel, or Lebanon seemed to be in the
offing.[39]

Thus, it seems a considerable oversimplification to assert that Soviet penetration of the Middle East prevents a replay of "Lebanon 1958." "Jordan 1970"
suggested that the United States could still land marines on a friendly Mediterranean shore. Washington is unlikely to undertake such an operation, but that is
because the length of friendly Arab shore has almost disappeared and because
support for "carrier diplomacy" has been deeply eroded in the United States.[40]

Moscow's reluctance to interpose its forces between the Sixth Fleet and the
Middle Eastern landing point may be partly related to its realization that the
Soviet Squadron is not yet an effective war-fighting force. If the function of the
Squadron in confrontation with the Sixth Fleet were that of a tripwire alone,
keeping the U.S. forces at arm's length would seem to require only a token
presence and the assurance of escalation to central war. But a tripwire is a crude
as well as dangerous policy instrument. It can be safely used only where the
other side can be relied on, with utmost confidence, to perceive both the "vital"
nature of the interest being defended and the certainty of a nuclear response if
shooting breaks out. Since these conditions are not likely to hold in most
conceivable scenarios, Moscow might consider the military defects of its Mediterranean forces as a significant weakness of its regional posture.

Whether Soviet policy would be emboldened by repairing the major gap of air
cover remains to be seen.[41] One suspects that even under these conditions, the
perception of relative interests and degree of resolve would still be critical. It
remains an elementary but still valid proposition that the "disutility" of nuclear
conflict weighs so heavily in the calculation of its expected "value" that
subjective probabilities of nuclear war have to be small indeed for confrontations
to be risked. It is necessary to stress the equally elementary point that only
subjective probabilities are relevant. The possibility of divergences between

[39] Presumably, Saudi Arabia is in the same class of protected clients, but this is not the place
for a discussion of Persian Gulf contingencies.
[40] It should be emphasized that the argument is only with the respect to the feasibility of
U.S. intervention without Soviet interference; whether intervention would be the best
course of action under the circumstances is another matter.
[41] Operation from Egyptian bases before July 1972 was, at best, only a partial solution of
the air-cover problem.
   The Soviet capability for intervention has been enhanced by the development of its
military airlift. According to Drew Middleton (*The New York Times,* 26 October 1973),
approximately 100 Antonov-22 long-range transports make up the core of this force.
Soviet airborne troops are supposed to have grown from seven divisions in 1971 to twelve
or thirteen now, with a total mobilized strength of 85–100 thousand men.

subjective and objective probabilities contributes to making our era more "interesting," in the sense in which the ancient Chinese would wish for their enemies to live in "interesting" times.

These issues are central to the outcome of the most dangerous Soviet-American confrontation scenarios, those developing from the resumption of large-scale fighting along the Middle Eastern cease-fire line. The dangers were muted in the October 1973 round of the Arab-Israeli war, largely because of the surprising effectiveness of the Arab forces, especially of their missile air-defense systems, which prevented the IDF from mounting sustained air attacks on rear areas. Therefore, one much-feared confrontation scenario, featuring a Soviet response to Israeli deep-penetration counterattacks that then evoked U.S. intervention, was obviated from the start. In its sharp response on October 24–25, the Nixon Administration may have prevented a Soviet intervention to break the Israeli stranglehold on an Egyptian force isolated on the East Bank. However, Washington called the worldwide alert not to force the capitulation of the Egyptians—Kissinger is reported to have told a visitor shortly after the crisis that he had no desire to see the Israelis take 70 thousand Egyptian prisoners—but to deter the introduction of a substantial Soviet military presence that, by its threat to the integrity of the IDF, might compel more direct counterinvolvement on the part of the United States.[42]

The Soviet reaction to the tough stand of the United States on October 24–25 was also in character. There was a total absence of bluster in Moscow. Instead, the setback was accepted with little visible irritation[43] and a cool denial that the USSR had any of the intentions ascribed to it in Washington. Given the American commitment to preserving the cease-fire and the Egyptian foothold on the East Bank, formalized in a U.N. compromise resolution the next day, the Soviet stake and therefore Moscow's defeat were diminished.

However, the relatively smooth disposition of this problem is no guarantee that the next crisis along the canal or on the Syrian heights will be resolved without Soviet direct intervention. Only if the political-military context remains unchanged—that is, if the calculations in both Washington and Moscow of relative interest, power, and determination continue to appear as they did in 1970–1973—is it likely that the Soviet decision will not be significantly altered. Deterrence is not an automatic mechanism in the system of Soviet-American interactions in the Middle East. The metaphor should perhaps be biological

[42] The Kremlin first suggested joint U.S.-Soviet intervention to force the Israelis to back off. Had the administration not insisted on the deletion from the Nixon-Brezhnev agreement of June 22, 1973, of a clause committing the sides to joint intervention anywhere in the world where the danger of nuclear conflict arose (Flora Lewis, *The New York Times,* 22 July 1973.), the script on October 24–25 might have read differently.
[43] Except, perhaps, at President Nixon's disclosure of an exchange of toughly worded messages between himself and Leonid Brezhnev. *The New York Times* 27 and 28 October 1973.

rather than mechanical: a plant to be nurtured and watched over, not a machine that can be programmed and then safely left unsupervised.

IV. The Politics of Confrontation Avoidance

The record of Soviet-American interaction in the Middle East, beginning with the 1967 crisis, demonstrates a far more pronounced interest by both powers in avoiding mutual confrontation than in marching to the brink in pursuit of particular regional objectives. Given the still primitive state of mechanics of Soviet-American consultation, which must be largely related to the ideological awkwardness of their rapprochement, the business of skirting the whirlpool of superpower conflict is conducted mainly in relations between the superpowers and their regional clients. For Moscow, this has involved, since the June War, its ties with Egypt, as contrasted with the pivotal role of Syria before that war.

For five years after the June debacle, Moscow had been counseling patience and faith in the ultimate efficacy of the strategy of "political solution." Cairo's confidence in its Soviet mentors had been wearing thin for some time (at least since March 1971[44]) but sounds of despair over the prolongation of the "crime" of "no war, no peace"[45] became audibly loud in the spring of 1972.[46] Heykal, in a burst of poetic emotion, demanded that "the calm which now crouches over the area like a nightmare should disperse, the whizzing of bullets should be heard, and the flames of fire should be seen soaring from afar."[47] The failure of the Moscow summit meeting to promise a political means of restoring the Sinai to Egypt, expected though that failure may have been, heightened Cairo's agitation. When it became clear, as Sadat contemptuously put it, that Moscow "would not fight," Cairo expelled the Soviet air and ground forces.

That the USSR was anxious to avoid a military confrontation with the United States over the conflict of their clients' interests had not been a secret to any Egyptian leader after the shock of being "abandoned" by Moscow during the Six-Day War. But the hardness of that fact of life remained to be tested and thoroughly appreciated. On the morrow of the June War, Cairo looked to a replay of the 1956 denouement—evacuation of the Israeli forces under combined Soviet-American pressure. The disappointment of that expectation, when Lyn-

---

[44] See the excerpts from Sadat's speech at a closed meeting of Egyptian newspaper publishers, published in *Newsweek*, 7 August 1972. After the purge of the Ali Sabry faction in May 1971, and the Egyptian intervention in support of General Numeiry's crushing of a Communist coup in Sudan in July, Heykal warned of Soviet estrangement: Arab relations with the Soviet Union had to be improved "without the least delay." *Al-Ahram*, 27 August 1971.

[45] See Heykal's columns in *al-Ahram* of 16, 23, 30 June, and 7 July 1972.

[46] For example, Sadat's May Day speech (Cairo Radio, 3 May 1972) and his replies to questions from members of the Central Committee of the Arab Socialist Union (*al-Akhbar*, 25 April 1972). See also the report of a seminar on the Moscow summit meeting in *al-Ahram*, 19 May 1972.

[47] *Al-Ahram*, 9 June 1972.

don Johnson refused to emulate Dwight Eisenhower, forced Nasser to turn to a strategy designed to raise the price to the Israelis of continued occupation of the conquered territories—to raise it to unacceptable levels. Thus was born the strategem of the War of Attrition, with its natural foundation in Soviet artillery tactics and weapons supply.

The overall Egyptian conception was attractively simple. It was true that the Soviet Union would not back an effort to eliminate the State of Israel: "The USSR, because of its world responsibilities, could not support us in this because such support would mean it would have to be prepared for nuclear war with the United States."[48] But Soviet military support was available for a "political solution," "eliminating the consequences of the 1967 aggression," because Washington could not unconditionally endorse Israeli occupation of the captured territories.[49] Between the hammer of Arab military blows and the anvil of Great-Power pressure, Israel would be forced to accept an Arab-favored settlement. Cairo expected, as Heykal suggested delicately, that "success in imposing a political solution . . . will create in the entire area and its vicinity a new situation whose effects on the future cannot yet be predicted."[50]

The realization of the "political solution" depended on successful prosecution of the War of Attrition, but that was seriously threatened by the IDF's employment of air power as a counterartillery weapon from the second half of 1969. A left-wing periodical quotes "one of the principal makers of Egyptian policy . . . , a man who was continually at the side of the *Rais* during these years and who enjoyed his total confidence," as saying that Nasser then decided to "transform the Israeli-Arab conflict into a Soviet-American one," to secure "Soviet military engagement at Egypt's side."[51] In the first half of 1970, Nasser undoubtedly felt that he had secured concrete physical assurance that the Soviets would not allow another Egyptian disaster. But having paused for a breather in August, Nasser had not yet tested the limits of Soviet readiness to intervene directly in the military conflict. It was left to his successor to learn the unpleasant truth.

The inevitable crisis was delayed for eighteen months. In part, the delay may be explained by the Egyptian fascination with exotic tools of war. Moscow was pressed to supply surface-to-surface missiles or MIG-25s and fobbed Cairo off with one excuse or another.[52] The issue of whether Soviet forces would directly

[48] Heykal in *al-Ahram*, 3 December 1970.
[49] Cf. Kissinger's oft-cited distinction (from a background briefing in June 1970) between defending Israel's existence and protecting Israel's 1967 conquests.
[50] *Al-Ahram*, 10 March 1972.
[51] Simon Malley, "L'engagement soviétique en Egypte," *Africasia* (December 7, 1970): 12-13. Compare Heykal: "Nasser succeeded in heightening the danger of the conflict from the local to the international level through his secret visit to the USSR in January 1970." *Al-Ahram*, 7 July 1972.
[52] See the report of Sadat's unpublished speech in *Newsweek*, 7 August 1972. In his second report on the expulsion to the Central Committee of the Arab Socialist Union on July 24, Sadat summarized the Soviet response to his repeated requests during his visits to Moscow: "They say, yes, yes, yes, to make things easy for us, but then we are caught in a whirlwind." *The New York Times*, 25 July 1972.

support an Egyptian attempt to recapture all or part of the Sinai was probably never posed bluntly, and the Soviets managed in a series of ambiguous statements to appear to be promising more far-reaching support than they were actually prepared to provide. Politburo Candidate-Member Boris Ponomarev, in Cairo on December 11, 1970, pledged that the Soviet Union would "support the struggle of the people and the leaders of the United Arab Republic under all circumstances."[53] Almost exactly a year later, *al-Goumhouriya* quoted Soviet Ambassador V. M. Vinogradov in a more explicit pledge: "If it is to be war, we will support you so that it will be a war with minimum losses."[54]

Moreover, the Kremlin's political support was unstinting on the key issues of the Middle Eastern crisis. One example was arms control. Although control of arms supply to Israel and the Arabs was constantly urged by the United States as an important means of avoiding superpower confrontation in the region, Moscow turned a deaf ear to such suggestions. Washington's appeal for restraint was denounced as misdirected and hypocritical, considering the sizable military support it provided Israel.[55] Soviet military assistance to the Arab states was in the interests of peace because it was directed to deterring or repelling Israeli aggression.[56] Until a political settlement is reached, Brezhnev told the twenty-fourth Party Congress, the USSR would "continue its firm support of its Arab friends." After a settlement, "we feel there could be a consideration of further steps designed for a military détente in the whole area, in particular for converting the Mediterranean into a sea of peace and friendly cooperation."[57] Two months later, Brezhnev declared: "We have never considered it an ideal situation to have the fleets of the great powers spending long periods cruising far away from their own shores. We are prepared to resolve this problem, but, as the phrase goes, on equal terms."[58]

Evidently, the Politburo was not merely defending Egyptian interests in rejecting U.S. regional arms-control initiatives. Consolidation of the Soviet position in the Middle East was obviously a concurrent objective. While Brezhnev hinted at mutual limitations on the superpower deployments, Soviet sources also insisted that since the Black Sea connects to the Mediterranean, the USSR is by definition and right a Mediterranean naval power.[59] Washington may have viewed arms control in the Middle East as a means of limiting the supply of sophisticated weaponry to the states of the region, but in Moscow it was asserted that "any projects directed to dispelling tension [in the region] would not achieve their goal and would, in fact, yield the opposite result, if they were to

---

[53] *The New York Times*, 13 December 1970.
[54] Cited in *The New York Times*, 17 December 1971.
[55] For example, V. Petrusenko, in *Pravda*, 15 March 1972.
[56] For example, D. Vol'skii, in *Izvestiia*, 17 February 1972.
[57] *Pravda*, 31 March 1971.
[58] *Pravda*, 12 June 1971.
[59] M. Petrov, "Proiski voenshchiny SShA na 'iuzhnom flange NATO'," *Kommunist vooruzhennykh sil* (no. 18, Sept. 1971):82.

ignore or leave untouched the imperialist position of strength in the Mediterranean—in the form of bases, fleets and military alliance systems."[60]

So, too, the Soviet Union fully supported and encouraged Egypt in the latter's
insistence on an Israeli commitment to full withdrawal from all occupied territories
before Cairo would enter into the interim arrangement the U.S. State Department
was promoting in 1971.[61] Since the new American initiative involved reopening
the Suez Canal, it might be thought that the Kremlin would be attracted to the
proposal. But Moscow gave every evidence of shunning the bait, evidently because it feared the hook of U.S. sponsorship.[62] The Kremlin was certainly not
anxious to provoke a showdown with its major Middle Eastern client.

Having secured Sadat's signature on the Treaty of Friendship on May 27,
1971, whose seventh article called for regular consultation and concerting
policy, Moscow may have thought it also obtained Sadat's recognition of the
wisdom of Soviet leadership. Perhaps it was this misplaced confidence that
induced the Kremlin to call the Egyptians' bluff and declare publicly, on the
occasion of the Moscow visits of Sadat in April and Sidky in July 1972, its belief
that Cairo now had the right to use any and all means to recapture the occupied
territory.[63] But Sadat had signed a piece of paper in exchange for some
advanced hardware and the prospect of direct Soviet involvement, and when
neither package was forthcoming he was not loath to demonstrate how little his
signature had meant.

Though it was doubtless stung by the unexpected blow, the Kremlin took a
long view. Sadat really had nowhere else to turn; sooner or later he (or a
successor) would have to return to the fold. Where else would Cairo find the
arms supply (even with the limitations Sadat publicly decried), the economic
aid, and the political support the USSR granted so unstintingly? The United
States was inextricably linked to Israeli "expansionism" in defense of "imperialist" positions in the Middle East, and Sadat would find only crumbs distrib-
uted from Washington's table.[64]

[60] Ia. Bronin, "Problemy sredizemnomoriia i imperialisticheskaia strategiia", *Mirovaia
ekonomika i mezhdunarodnye otnosheniia* (no. 9, September 1971):25.

[61] See, for example, the Riad-Gromyko communique in *Pravda,* 5 July 1971. See also V.
Nekrasov (deputy chief editor of *Pravda*), on Radio Moscow, 6 June 1971; and E.
Primakov, in *Pravda,* 5 January 1972.

[62] For evidence of Soviet suspicions that some Egyptians were succumbing to the American
lures, see E. Primakov, in *Pravda,* 5 June 1971; and R. Petrov, "Step Towards Arab
Unity," *New Times* (no. 35, September 1971):22.

[63] *Pravda,* 30 April and 15 July 1972.

[64] Apart from whatever hopes he may have entertained of inducing the Kremlin to become
more aggressive in his behalf, Sadat's move to expel his mentors may have been motivated
also by fears and hopes pertaining to U.S. policy. U.S.–Israeli relations were becoming
overtly and progressively warmer after Prime Minister Meir's visit to Washington in
December 1971, and Sadat may have felt that an opening to the West had to be broken
through before it was too late. But he either failed to prepare the ground adequately or
had grossly overestimated his cards. What awaited him in Washington was only mild
encouragement and the demand for "proximity" negotiations which could easily be
transformed into direct negotiations.

If Cairo repented, would not Moscow welcome back its prodigal? Egypt remained the most populous, the most powerful of Arab states—the natural leader of the Arab world. No change of stance or regime could affect Egypt's geostrategic position at the hinge of Asia and Africa. Four centuries earlier Henri IV thought conversion to Catholicism a small price to pay for a unified French monarchy: Paris was worth a Mass. When the break came, the Kremlin evidently believed retention of a Soviet position in Egypt was worth ingesting its pride, and bided its time.[65]

Rather than risk being dragged along by its desperate client into confrontation with U.S. power, Moscow accepted the humiliation of expulsion with dignity and studied indifference. In the framework of the worldwide alliance of anti-imperialist forces, a Soviet foreign-policy commentator had noted some six weeks before, "each of its participants, while struggling for the solution of common tasks and for progress toward common objectives, takes its own path—namely, the path that most fully corresponds with particular features of its situation and which is in accordance with its opportunities." The Soviet Union's contribution to the general revolutionary cause and its "revolutionary duty" includes the pursuit "of a policy of peace, the peaceful coexistence of countries with different social systems, and of relaxation of international tension."[66]

Moscow refused to be tied to the principle that it must toughen its position in response to "one or another tough action by imperialism." "The strength of socialist policy has never lain in primitiveness and stereotype, and even less in an identical repetition of the modes and methods used by the class enemy." Soviet foreign policy combines "a firm rebuff to imperialism's aggressive actions with great flexibility in the approach to one or another disputed problem." Its watchword is "principled firmness and tactical flexibility." Almost as if he were speaking directly to Egyptian critics of Soviet policy, the commentator warned against the short-sightedness that prevented "a correct combination of current immediate tasks of the present with the long-term prospects and objectives of the future. . . . The revolutionary of the present never lives by the interests solely of the present."[67]

Whatever private suspicions it may have had that such was the basic Soviet attitude, Washington long felt unsure that an Egyptian attempt to embroil the USSR in another Middle East war would not succeed. Hence, up to 1972, the fear of confrontation with the USSR in the Middle East had been a major goad

---

[65] It did not have too long to wait. The first Soviet military delegation to visit Egypt after the 1972 break arrived in Cairo on February 12, 1973. After the October War, the Arabs would be reminded of the military cooperation article in the Soviet Egyptian Treaty of May 1971: "During those days of October, the world witnessed the fruits of this cooperation" (Radio Moscow in Arabic, 30 October 1973).

[66] Vadim Zagladin, "Printsipal'nost' i posledovatel'nost'," *Novoe vremia* (no. 22, May 26, 1972):4—5.

[67] *Ibid.*, p. 5.

to U.S. policy makers. Of the possible avenues to reducing the danger of confrontation, the United States patiently and persistently explored two of the three: (*1*) reducing the danger of resumption of war between Israel and the Arab states; (*2*) diminishing the incentive of the USSR to involve itself directly on the side of Egypt or Syria if war broke out.

Washington's efforts concentrated on the first of these approaches, largely by seeking to promote a settlement of the underlying conflict, but also by attempting to preserve a "balance of power" in the region to deter an Arab attack on Israel. Unable to secure Soviet agreement to a joint limitation on the flow of sophisticated weapons to the region, the Nixon Administration reluctantly but periodically reinforced the IDF. The second approach involved occasional warnings to Moscow about the dangers of adventurist action, but was largely based on the maintenance of the Sixth Fleet in the area and the lasting effect of the Fleet's maneuvering in the Eastern Mediterranean in the fall of 1970.

A third possibility would be to weaken the U.S. commitment to Israel's defense.[68] But five years of concern with growing Soviet power in the Mediterranean and frequent spells of fear that the fuse of the Middle Eastern "powder keg" was sputtering did not bring the United States to disassociate itself from Israel. Indeed, the warmth of the tie in 1972 was at an all-time peak. Yet the euphoria was of recent origin. Was it also fated to be of brief duration? A summary review of one of the major crisis points in U.S.-Israel relations— December 1969—may highlight the important planes of friction between the two countries, then and now.

In December 1969, the revelation of the Rogers Plan for Israel-Egypt and Israel-Jordan arrangements, in the words of a *New York Times* report (22 December 1969), "provoked what appears to be the gravest crisis of confidence between the United States and Israel in nine months of international peacemaking efforts." It was, in fact, the gravest crisis of confidence in the thirty months that had elapsed since the Six-Day War. Not since the Eisenhower Administration pressured Israel into withdrawing from Sinai and Gaza in early 1957 had there been such bitterness in Israel over American policy. Mrs. Meir's vehement rejection of the American proposals—declaring that it would be "treasonous" for any Israeli government to accept them, accusing the United States of "appeasement"—were unprecedented in their public explicitness.

An observer on the sidelines, noting the other side's reaction to previous settlement proposals, might have wondered at the heat of the Israeli response.

[68] Pressure on Israel may be envisioned in other forms but their ultimate effect is on the informal U.S. guarantee of Israel's survival. This is true even of financial pressures—for example, cutting off economic aid or removing the tax-exempt status of private donations. It is inconceivable that such actions could be taken without at least affecting others' perceptions of U.S. readiness to ward off threats to Israel's security, and most likely they would be possible only if significant changes occurred in U.S. Government and public views on U.S.-Israeli relations.

Rejection of the current set of proposals by the Arabs and the Soviets seemed in the cards, and Israel might have saved itself the pain of rubbing its only important friend the wrong way. Israelis, however, were not concerned about Soviet or Arab acceptance of the proposals then on the table; indeed, rejection by all sides was seen as inevitable in Jerusalem as well. The note of anguish in Israel's response was evoked by fear of further erosion of the American position under the pressure of the Arabs, the "oil interests," and the Four-Power negotiations.

In the aftermath of the Six-Day War, Jerusalem was delighted to discover that far from wanting to repeat the 1957 experience, when Israel was pressured into evacuating Sinai and the Gaza Strip with only the vaguest "understanding" about an Egyptian *quid pro quo,* the Johnson Administration backed the Israeli strategy of trading territory for a "real peace." Jerusalem and Washington shared the conviction that the 1949 armistice arrangements were no longer tolerable and that the time had come to settle only for a directly negotiated, contractual peace treaty. By the time it left office, the Johnson Administration had weakened its position considerably, and its adherence to the basic postulate of peace through direct negotiations could no longer be assumed. This was manifest in the November 1968 Rusk proposal for an Egyptian-Israeli settlement. It evoked little public reaction at the time, only because it was confidential and because it was rejected by the Egyptians out of hand.

The conditions operating to move the Johnson Administration off center in its waning days were essentially those that induced the incoming Nixon Administration to take a new policy direction. The disaster of June 1967 had not brought the Arabs around; the year-long mediation efforts of Gunnar Jarring had been fruitless; the Russians had replaced all the Arabs' material losses and more; the Fedayeen were becoming an important force on their own; most importantly, the cease-fire lines had become intermittent-fire lines with the ever-present threat that the cycle of attack and reprisal would escalate into a full-fledged war into which the superpowers might be sucked willy-nilly. Seeing, as well, an increasing danger to U.S. relations with its remaining friends in the Arab world (the conservative monarchies and Lebanon) the Nixon Administration turned to Great Power negotiations to work out a settlement before it was too late. In entering the talks, Washington was aware of the dangers of failure and estimated only limited probabilities of success, but it counted on a presumptive Soviet interest in preventing a fourth round in the Middle East. Above all, the Nixon Administration felt that the costs of continued inaction outweighed those of the new direction.

From the very beginning, Israel made no secret of its absolute opposition to the Great Power talks. The talks were not being conducted on how to get the parties to the conference table where they would themselves settle their dispute, but on what piece of paper to put before them. By definition, the Great Power talks were a rejection of the principle of direct negotiation of all elements of a peace agreement. Washington maintained that the talks were intended only to establish a basis for negotiations, and it continued to recognize the importance of a contractual agreement arrived at directly between the parties. However, Israel came increasingly to believe that the Americans no longer held a commitment to the principle of a directly negotiated peace, only to the need for some kind of settlement soon.

There was a fundamental disagreement between Washington and Jerusalem centering on the validity of the half-loaf analogy. The Rogers Plan did not call for *de jure* recognition of Israel but recognition of its "sovereignty, territorial integrity, political independence, and right to live in peace." Securing Arab agreement to this formula was viewed in the State Department as a formidable but not impossible job, provided Israel made the appropriate concessions. An arrangement based on this formula could be a durable settlement, which would ultimately be transformed into normal state-to-state relations. However, formal recognition was out of the question, and if that was the price of a settlement, none would be obtained. But to Jerusalem, which continued to regard the Arab-Israeli conflict as a confrontation over Israel's right to exist, substantive concessions made sense only in response to a demonstrable reversal of Arab attitudes. Only when the Arabs agreed to face Israel across a bargaining table would it be clear that they were at last prepared to live in peace with the Jewish state.

The principle of negotiation was the first casualty of the Four-Power talks, declared Mrs. Meir to the Knesset in December 1969. In the Israeli view there were bound to be others, for the U.S. role in the talks was anomalous. Hoping to play the part of evenhanded go-between, Washington found itself instead in the uncomfortable role of pleader of Israel's cause to balance unambiguous Soviet partisanship. As the Arab pressures on the United States to change policy mounted, it was only natural that the United States would try to escape being tarred with the brush of pro-Israelism by adopting a policy consciously different from Israel's.

There was a dilemma in the American approach to a Middle East settlement that had not escaped Soviet observation. On one hand, there is a strand in U.S. thinking that harks back to the pre-Six-Day War support for the "territorial integrity of all states in the region." This is the principle recorded in Security Council Resolution 242 of November 1967 "emphasizing the inadmissibility of the acquisition of territory by war." On the other hand, there was a residual support of the strategy of no withdrawal without peace and of the Israeli demand for secure and recognized borders, although the position had been impaired by a somewhat more elastic view of the requirements of "peace" and the definition of "security." Hence, the Soviet accusation that the United States wished "to turn the unconditional demand for the evacuation of the occupied Arab lands into a subject for barter" was disconcerting. The tension of operating under that dilemma was an additional eroding force.

As it viewed the U.S. alarm over the consequences of close identification with Israel and the "explosive" situation on the cease-fire lines, Jerusalem grimly speculated on the approaching showdown with its sponsor, on the likelihood that Washington would cut Israel off to face the Soviets and the Arabs unaided. Fear of abandonment by the United States was a recurrent nightmare of the Israeli political imagination. Even when American support was least stinting, there was an underlying uneasiness that the foundations of that support were built on sand. Jerusalem had often attempted to convince Washington that Israel was the most effective counter to Soviet penetration, but the State Department was only partly impressed, being far more concerned about the danger to U.S. interests in Jordan, Lebanon, Saudi Arabia, and the Persian Gulf. Israel had lived for two decades with the conviction that it was an unwanted child, that the optimum solution to the Arab-Israeli conflict from the State Department's point of view was the sudden and quiet disappearance of the Jewish state from the Middle East map. Israelis argued that the radicalization of the Arab world, which was accompanied by the progressive diminution of U.S. presence and influence in the region, was historically inevitable and only tangentially related to the Arab-Israeli conflict. But they were not able to convince their listeners. Since no one had yet thought up a compelling rationale for the strategic necessity of an American alliance with Israel, there was a nagging fear that some day, to defend interests perceived as vital, the United States would be ready to sell Israel down the Persian Gulf.

Notes of strident tension in U.S.–Israel relations were not confined to the period of 1969–1970. After the breakdown of the Jarring talks in February 1971, brought about by Israel's refusal to commit itself to complete withdrawal in advance of negotiations with the Arabs, Washington began an active effort to bring Israel and Egypt together in an interim agreement that would reopen the Suez Canal and move Israeli troops back into Sinai.[69] These discussions were marked by a number of acrimonious exchanges, particularly during Secretary Rogers' visit to Israel in May 1971. As late as December 1971, Mrs. Meir felt it necessary to journey to Washington for a personal meeting with President Nixon to clear the atmosphere.

The atmospheric change in 1972 was indeed surprising. Imposition of a settlement on Israel now seemed to be the farthest thing from Washington's mind. Both sides chose to ignore past unpleasantness and the 1969 Rogers Plan

[69] The implicit abandonment of the principle of "no withdrawal without peace" was Israeli-initiated. It was Dayan who broached the notion first, before it was taken up in Cairo and Washington.

was treated with the delicacy reserved for the peccadillos of a family black sheep newly restored to grace.[70] Now, military and political support of Israel was the order of the day. The then Israeli Ambassador in Washington, Yitzhak Rabin, extolled the Republican Administration in terms that aroused a flurry of controversy in the United States: "I do not recall that any previous U.S. President undertook commitments as President Nixon did during his speech to the joint meeting of the two Houses of Congress after the Moscow talks, when he said: 'I reemphasized to the Russians the American people's commitment to safeguard the existence of the State of Israel'."[71]

If in mid-1972 relations between the United States and Israel were at a level that evoked enthusiastic political support for the Administration from the Israeli Embassy in Washington, was it not due in part to Israel's intransigence, Jerusalem wondered aloud? Twice in President Nixon's first term, the U.S. government withheld sales of advanced jet aircraft to Israel—during the spring and summer of 1970 and again in the latter half of 1971. Neither episode brought any perceptible softening of the Israeli stand[72] (or any apparent diminution in the scale of Soviet involvement and in the flow of Soviet weaponry to the region). Lurking in the background of any possible U.S. calculation of the leverage that could be exerted on Israel by granting or withholding arms was the threat of an Israeli nuclear potential. It did not seem possible to pressure Israel by withholding arms, at least not without incurring high political costs.

Perhaps most important, the effort seemed unnecessary. The twin specters that had exercised Washington's imagination and had driven the State Department to intensive bouts of diplomatic effort, superpower confrontation and polarization, were seemingly exorcised. Negotiations with Moscow had revealed that the Kremlin's fear of confrontation, contrary to the original expectation of the Nixon Administration, was considerably weaker than the concern for the maintenance of the Soviet position in the Arab world. Washington's own fears of the consequences of another round of Arab-Israeli war were attenuated as the cease-fire on the canal held and Cairo demonstrated its unwillingness to resume the battle. The crushing defeat of the Fedayeen in Jordan had removed the

---

[70] Cf. the following comments by Yosef Harif, an Israeli journalist known for the accuracy of his reports of supposedly confidential cabinet proceedings: "Everybody in Washington knows that [the Rogers Plan] is dead, although no one is thinking, in the expression of a senior American official, of arranging a 'public requiem.' A White House figure was prepared to say only this: 'The Rogers Plan is history. We are not annulling it; we are not confirming it. It certainly does not obligate the United States, with respect to either the USSR or Egypt, on the question of borders.' He also said: 'If they will come now and say, we now agree to what we rejected before, we will tell them—now [the Rogers plan] doesn't obligate us. The principle is that the *borders must be determined in negotiations between the sides.*" Maariv, 15 December 1972.

[71] In an interview on Israeli radio, 10 June 1972.

[72] The Cabinet's decision in July 1970 to agree to withdrawal in some form, an action that brought about the resignation of the right-wing Gahal ministers, was surely motivated by the desire for a cease-fire rather than the hope for American arms.

threat to Hussein's throne and paralyzed the radicalizing force of militant Palestinian nationalism. Thus, even the massive responses of the IDF to periodic flare-ups of terrorist activity along the Lebanese and Syrian borders failed to evoke significant U.S. reactions. Nor did declarations such as that of the IDF's chief of staff, General Elazar, that Israel's desire to preserve the cease-fire was "no stronger than our desire and our iron determination to fight the saboteurs. Therefore, our desire to keep the cease-fire cannot deter us from operations against the saboteurs even if these operations endanger the cease-fire."[73]

Heykal noted with some bitterness that support of Israel had not harmed U.S. trade interests in the Middle East: U.S. exports to the Arab world had continued to increase, from $275 million in the first quarter of 1971 to $307 million in the first quarter of 1972.[74] As for the escalating demands of oil producers, through most of 1972 they seemed to reflect a dynamic of their own, only tangentially related to the Arab-Israeli conflict.

This is not to say that the United States and Israel reached complete accord in 1972 and certainly not on Israel's terms. Mrs. Meir was undoubtedly aware that, whether the 1969 Rogers Plan was alive or dead, in a renewed military crisis, Washington would still be attempting to distinguish between support for Israel's territorial conquests and commitment to its national existence. Ambassador Rabin followed his praise of President Nixon on the radio interview cited earlier with a grim caution: "On the other hand, I repeat that the lesson we learned on the eve of the Six-Day War should be imprinted in our minds and should remind us that when the die is cast and we face the test, we find ourselves alone, face to face with our fate."

When the die was cast on October 6, 1973, Israel found itself almost alone. Its political isolation was nearly complete, but large arms shipments from the United States contributed to the Israeli recovery from initial setbacks and helped keep the scale of casualties from reaching disastrous proportions. Washington's actions in the Yom Kippur War clearly reemphasized the Nixon Administration's policy distinction between defending Israel's conquests and preserving Israel's existence.

It was an event that even the pessimists in Israel failed to foresee that revived the strains in U.S.-Israel relations and may have been responsible for the outbreak of war itself. This was the linking of the Arab-Israeli conflict to the power struggle between the Middle Eastern oil countries and the major industrial consumers. Cairo overcame its inhibitions about attempting to cross the Suez Canal in force without direct Soviet involvement only after becoming convinced that there was no other way of breaking the stalemate except by making concessions that were still deemed too costly. But perhaps this was only the necessary condition and the sufficient one was the possibility of putting into

[73] *Maariv*, 3 November 1972.
[74] Heykal, in *al-Ahram*, 23 June 1972, citing U.S. Department of Commerce figures.

play the "oil weapon," to force the Nixon Administration to apply effective pressure on Israel. Were the military action and oil pressure inseparably linked in Cairo's view? On the eve of the war, a major Egyptian journalist seemed to hint at impending linkage: "We cannot expect anything from U.S. Secretary of State Henry Kissinger in regard to the crisis, without exerting pressure. Fruitful pressure cannot be confined to the oil pressure. We need to raise the level of pressure through action to end the deadlock."[75]

The long-sought opportunity to wield the "oil weapon" arrived only in 1973, as King Faisal of Saudi Arabia abandoned his longstanding insistence that oil and Arab-Israeli politics did not mix. Faisal's reversal of position came about as Saudi oil revenues, swollen by the combination of escalating prices and the sharp increases in Aramco's scale of production, outdistanced the Saudi capacity to consume or invest. With world demand for oil promising to be brisk into the eighties and nineties and the international monetary system in near-constant crisis, it became clear that oil in the ground was worth more than money in the bank. For the first time, Faisal could afford to become an active participant in the Arab "battle of destiny." Interruptions of supply, used as a weapon to pressure the supporters of Israel, would cost him nothing; with the world hungry for oil, the action would even add to his coffers.

So the conjuncture of events was favorable for joint Arab political-military action. Whether or not this included Saudi involvement in the strategic planning of the war,[76] the exacerbation of the energy crisis by the Arab embargo and production cutback, coupled with the results on the battlefield, seemed to move the Nixon Administration to energetic action in directions that Arabs found more favorable to their interests than did Israelis. His first call for a cease-fire on October 7, Kissinger is said to have assured Heykal, was expected "to be in [the Arab] interest before it could be in Israel's interest."[77] Jerusalem conditionally accepted the State Department's proposal for a cease-fire in place several days later, but with evident reluctance. The White House decided to counter the Soviet airlift with one to Israel, only after the failure of the cease-fire negotiations and then only for fear that serious weakening of the IDF might tempt its

---

[75] Ihsan Abd al-Quddus, chief editor of *Akhbar al-Yawm,* 29 September 1973.

[76] For an assertion of Saudi involvement, see Juan de Orris in *The New York Times,* 10 November 1973. An alternative view, that Sadat went to war in part to avoid becoming Faisal's compliant tool, is presented in the *Neue Zuricher Zeitung,* 12 October 1973. After the fact, an Egyptian journalist appeared to argue that an Israeli military defeat was necessary for the oil weapon to be credible: "Who guards the oil, the Arabs or Israel? If the oil remained just a raw material in shaky hands, then the second premise would be the correct one—namely, that Israel can defeat the Arabs and guard the oil. This is why the use of the oil weapon had to be concomitant with the fighting. The October War was necessary for the oil weapon to have a meaning." (Baha ad-Din, in *al-Ahram,* 3 November 1973.)

[77] *Al-Ahram,* 16 November 1973. Heykal was presumably referring to the U.S. call for a Security Council meeting. The council met the following day and Ambassador Scali proposed a cease-fire with return to the October 5 lines.

opponents to play for higher stakes than recovery of a piece of the Sinai desert.[78]

Jerusalem was effusively grateful for the literally lifesaving supplies.[79] However, the limited nature of the U.S. backing was demonstrated anew when Kissinger hastily flew to Moscow, within hours of a Brezhnev invitation, to work out a cease-fire that was intended to avert another disastrous defeat of Arab arms. As for the U.S. military alert on October 25, the alarm was occasioned by the prospect of Soviet forces attacking the IDF on the cease-fire line. Had the Kremlin actually dispatched troops, but explicitly with the purpose of protecting Cairo or Damascus, it is doubtful that the U.S. reaction would have exceeded verbal protests.

Both Washington and Jerusalem denied that pressure was being exerted on Israel, but as the peace conference was prepared, it was made clear to the Israelis that they were expected to agree to hand back just about all of the territory occupied in 1967 in return for which Washington might provide a unilateral or joint U.S.-Soviet guarantee. Perhaps the United States could cope with the Arab oil embargo, but, according to James Reston, Kissinger warned the Israelis that "the United States is not prepared to risk war with the Soviet Union every time there is an Arab-Israeli conflict, unless there is a clear violation of some internationally guaranteed agreement."[80]

V. The Aftermath of the October War

A crisis in international relations casts a powerful light on events of the time. As Laqueur has written, "all the quasi-problems suddenly disappear and . . . perception of the issues is sharpened . . . [a crisis] clears away the cobwebs of wishful thinking, of irrelevant theories and spurious explanations." However, he warns, "the danger of distortion is greatest at a time of crisis; . . . events which loom very large at the moment of writing may appear in a different perspective a few years later."[81]

The caution is well-taken. The analyst of current events has a natural tendency to project the trends of the recent past, a tendency that receives academic legitimation from contemporary theories of bureaucratic politics that emphasize the inertia of large organizations. In the wake of a crisis it is even more difficult

---

[78] According to Heykal (*ibid.*), Kissinger justified the U.S. aid to Israel as follows: "You can, of course, imagine the internal pressure we came under to help Israel. When we could not cope with the internal pressure through a Security Council decision to cease firing, we began to help Israel."

[79] Drew Middleton's report (*The New York Times*, 28 November 1973) that the volume of cargo delivered to Israel in the month following the war was only a tenth as large as that obtained by Syria and Egypt from the USSR in the same period is apparently incorrect. The flow to both sides was approximately equal in tonnage delivered.

[80] *The New York Times*, 9 December 1973, section 4.

[81] Walter Laqueur, *The Struggle for the Middle East*, (Baltimore, Md.: Penguin Books, 1972), p. 17.

to contemplate alternatives to the course emerging from the immediate experience. Nevertheless, we must beware, as Laqueur enjoins us, of "the cunning of reason: a great triumph may be the prelude to disaster and a defeat may eventually turn into victory."[82] The following comments on relations of the Great Powers with their clients and on the state of détente in the Middle East attempt to keep that injunction in mind.

June 1967 was a defeat for Soviet policy and Soviet-supplied arms but was followed by the appearance in Egypt and Syria of the largest Soviet military presence outside the Communist area and since the Bolshevik Revolution. Two years later the wheel turned full circle: The expulsion of the Soviet military from Egypt in July 1972 seemed to mark a dramatic break in the long line of the USSR's advance into the Middle East. Little more than a year later, Moscow was heavily involved again in aiding the military efforts of its major clients and in defending their political interests in various international forums.

Soviet fortunes have risen and fallen at various times since the USSR reappeared on the Middle East scene in the middle 1950s, but the net result up to the present time is surely unmistakable. During the first two decades after World War II, the USSR was unable to secure acceptance of its claim that the Middle East was a legitimate sphere of Soviet interest. Indeed, after the creation of the State of Israel, Moscow generally withdrew from involvement in the region until after Stalin's death. However, in the dozen years after the Egyptian-Czech arms agreement, Moscow gained and expanded a bridgehead in the Arab world, and helped trigger (but also control the spread of) the Six-Day War. That brief interval brought the USSR the historic achievement of recognition as one of the two arbiters of the region's destiny. Thus, in his address at the UN's twenty-fifth anniversary session on October 23, 1970, President Nixon acknowledged that "the Middle East is the place today . . . where the vital interests of the United States and the Soviet Union are both involved."[83] It is the United States and the USSR that are the effective cosponsors of the post-October peace negotiations.

During a quarter century of strife in the Middle East, the United States had failed to prevent the penetration of the region by the USSR or to secure its "rollback." One may point to a variety of particular factors in operation, including both U.S. errors and Soviet skill, but containment failed in the Middle East basically because the process depends on the existence of a strong will to resist on the part of the local states. In the Middle East, in sharp contrast to Western Europe, that will did not exist. On the contrary, the USSR found a significant confluence of its own interests with those of the radical elites that came to power in a number of Middle Eastern countries. In the period since the Six-Day War, Washington found that it was impossible to secure the agreement of the USSR to a broad-based settlement of the local conflict, because the

[82] *Ibid.*
[83] *The New York Times,* 24 October 1970.

dynamics of the situation seemed to Moscow to promise the expulsion of the
United States from the region entirely.

As Soviet involvement intensified, in 1969–1970, there were some who regarded the fundamental problem of the Middle Eastern crisis as one of assuring
the Soviet Union a legitimate place in the Middle East. (There were others who
wondered whether the Soviet Union could possibly be persuaded to legitimate
the U.S. position in the Middle East.) But the United States has not prevented
Soviet penetration in the Middle East; it could not "expel" the Soviet Union
from the Middle East; it could not offer Moscow "a place" in the Middle East.
Washington could either accede to Soviet penetration or try to contain its limits.

Nevertheless, the Soviet position proved vulnerable. My mid-1970 consideration of Soviet policy alternatives in the Middle East suggested the importance of
the level of Soviet control over the policy of its major client in determining the
outcome of Moscow's confrontation with high-risk, high-cost policy options.[84]
The paper concluded with the observation that "increasing Soviet involvement
without sufficient control could generate tensions that might be resolved at the
extremes of the spectrum, either less involvement or high-control greater involvement."[85] Evidently, at the crunch-point in July 1972, Moscow's control in
Egypt proved inadequate and Soviet forces withdrew without a struggle. The
Kremlin would undoubtedly prefer to get back into Egypt on terms that assured
much greater Soviet control, but that may prove impossible to obtain. Presumably, this will reinforce Moscow's inclination to limit its commitments
carefully.

If the USSR's position in Egypt today is less than perfectly assured, it reflects
a Soviet failure to steer the evolution of the state and society in a consistently
"progressive" direction. Old illusions about the pliability of the military revolutionaries have been dispelled. In a prophetic passage penned in 1968, Georgii
Mirskii, the Soviet specialist on the role of the military in underdeveloped
countries declared:

> The conception of the consistently progressive role of the army in Asia and
> Africa has turned out to be nothing more than an illusion. As the example of
> the Egyptian revolution has shown, the army is capable of playing a pro-
> gressive role at the stage of the liquidation of feudal rule as well as in the initial
> period of social transformation. But in the stage of profound social revolution,
> the army usually manifests conservative tendencies.[86]

Mirskii's reference to Egypt was to the officer class and the debacle of 1967.
He regarded Nasser himself as one of the outstanding examples of the small

[84] A. S. Becker, "Future Policy Alternatives" (pp. 605–636) of A. S. Becker and A. L.
Horelick, "Soviet Policy in the Middle East," in Hammond and Alexander, eds., *Political
Dynamics in the Middle East.*
[85] *Ibid.*, p. 636.
[86] Mirskii, "O kharaktere sotsial'nykh sil v Azii i Afrike," *Kommunist* (no. 17, 1968):96.

group of "revolutionary democrats with epaulettes"—the only category of third-world military leaders Mirskii considered "progressive."[87] But Nasser, the conspicuous exception, was gone, and Sadat turned out to be just another petit-bourgeois pragmatist.

Soviet wariness toward Sadat must be strengthened by the recent development of a Saudi-Egyptian common front. Relations between Moscow and Riyadh are now unusually smooth—for the first time, Faisal congratulated the USSR on the anniversary of the Bolshevik Revolution and the Soviets responded with appreciation[88] —but the increasingly assertive Saudi voice is still a conservative one that must be hostile to an expanding Soviet role in both the Eastern Mediterranean and the Persian Gulf.

It is Sadat, moreover, who chose to announce agreement to restore relations with the United States precisely on November 7, the anniversary of the Revolution. According to Heykal, Kissinger expressed his appreciation of the contrast between Egyptian actions after the October War and those after the June War: "In 1967 you stirred up the world against us . . . President al-Sadat acted more calmly in 1973 . . . you have opened the door for us to play a role we have the desire to perform and feel we can perform."[89]

But if the United States chose to walk through that door, it was in part because of the long-term pressure exerted by the USSR. The understanding expressed for the Arab position, the readiness to work for a settlement that requires near-total Israeli withdrawal came about because of the October War and its oil embargo aftermath. Moscow had little hand in the latter but had a clearly major role in the former. Heykal accused Kissinger of holding "the realities of power" foremost in his crisis calculations, and feared that "if Israel is able to change the conditions of power in the field, we could find ourselves required to accept these new conditions as a new basis." For Heykal, this underscored the importance of the global balance of power and hence of the Soviet role in the Middle East. "This role should not be secondary or a temporary element, but should be confirmed through deep Soviet-Arab understanding and long-lasting friendship."[90] Cairo may recognize that only the United States can secure Israeli withdrawal, but it will probably also continue to appreciate that only the Soviet Union can keep the United States interested in securing that withdrawal.

There is then reason to suppose that the USSR will retain an important position in Egypt, failing a basic resolution of the Arab-Israeli conflict. In recent years Moscow has shown increasing interest in Persian Gulf affairs as well, developing a close and special relationship with Iraq. This development and the centrality of South Asia in Soviet designs for the containment of China place

[87] Mirskii, *Armiia i politika v stranakh Azii i Afriki,* (Moscow: Nauka, 1970), p. 304.
[88] As an example, on Radio Moscow in Arabic, 13 November 1973.
[89] *Al-Ahram,* 16 November 1973.
[90] *Ibid.*

Soviet interests in the Eastern Mediterranean in altered perspective. Calvocoressi has observed that the in-betweenness of the Middle East was its salient characteristic for British policy in the imperial era. The Middle East was important because Europe's trade with the East was important, and the Middle East was the passageway from the English Channel to the Indian Ocean.[91] As Calvocoressi also noted, the region serves a similar function for the Soviet Union.[92] The significance of the Middle East in Soviet policy would increase considerably as Soviet interests in the Persian Gulf and Indian Ocean matured. The latter could also be associated with a redirection of emphasis away from Egypt and the Eastern Mediterranean, but at an evident cost.

With the death of Nasser, Moscow lost an important fulcrum for its leverage in the Arab and in much of the underdeveloped world too. Egypt could be expected to continue to play a major role in inter-Arab affairs by virtue of its size and Soviet-supplied power, but that role would be unlikely to serve Soviet interests nearly so well as in the past. Egypt's future strategic value could be seen from Moscow as having two components: one related to countering the U.S. power in the Mediterranean, an aspect already discussed at length, but the other was connected to Egypt's command of the artery linking the Mediterranean and the Arabian Sea.

For several years, Moscow was content to leave this bright promise unrealized. Soviet leaders were not sufficiently concerned about the continued closure of the Suez Canal to be willing to join Cairo in an attempt to push the Israelis out of the Bar-Lev line. As one consequence of the October War, the exploitation of that opportunity may be at hand, if an agreement for at least partial Israeli withdrawal in the Sinai can be negotiated.

In the waning days of 1973, the conditions for settlement, and perhaps the basic objectives as well, of Arabs and Israelis, seemed as difficult to reconcile as ever before. So long as Israel remains in control of large sections of pre-Six-Day War Arab territory, each cease-fire must be viewed with foreboding in Arab capitals. Well before the October War it had been a widespread view in Cairo that Egypt's only hope was, in Heykal's words, to "set ablaze a region in which the world will not allow any fire." Heykal assumed then, as perhaps the October War reinforced the belief among others, that "even fire has different degrees of temperature which can be precisely and expertly controlled."[93] In December 1973, the third post-Six-Day War cease-fire was formally holding but artillery on both fronts was active daily. A new flare-up of October dimensions seemed far from improbable.

Concerned to head off a fifth round of the Arab-Israeli war, Washington has publicly recognized the reality of both Arab frustration with the *status-quo-ante*

[91] Peter Calvocoressi, "Britain and the Middle East," in Hammond and Alexander, eds., *Political Dynamics in the Middle East,* pp. 425–426.
[92] *Ibid.,* p. 439.
[93] *Al-Ahram,* 23 June 1972.

October and Israel's fears for its security within shrunken borders. However, the mechanism to bridge the gap between the two realities—international guarantees—has never aroused Israeli enthusiasm and is less likely to do so now than ever before. True, Israel's political isolation is almost complete and only the United States remains a friend among the major powers. But while the United States is indeed Israel's best and only significant friend, their interests often diverge. A major case in point is oil, and a renewed Arab embargo in the future might find the United States more heavily dependent on external sources and therefore more reluctant to bear the costs of maintaining its support for Israel.

Other reasons for Israeli skepticism are also apparent. With the best will in the world on both sides, the credibility of an American guarantee has been tarnished by domestic upheavals. Part of the problem is obviously a legacy of the Vietnam involvement, but the "no-more-Vietnams" syndrome only strengthens Israeli doubts on the likelihood of immediate U.S. response if ever Jeruslaem invoked the promise of assistance. Even if it were forthcoming, the effectiveness of a U.S. response to an ally thousands of miles away and having no strategic depth can be legitimately questioned.

There has always been a tension in U.S.-Israeli relations caused by Washington's sense of frustration that it has incurred the onus of identification with Israel without the compensating advantage of influencing major policy decisions in Jerusalem. For its part, the latter feels constrained to resist U.S. pressure so long as American action in Israel's behalf is improvised and scenario-dependent rather than defined in a long-term alliance framework. Viewed from Jerusalem, the likelihood of such an overt U.S.-Israeli alliance is poor, largely for the reasons already indicated, but also because the probability of the United States enduring in easy alliance with any one else is also poor. Observing the rocky course of U.S.–West European relations, a thoughtful Israeli might consider the Europeans fortunate that no significant present danger threatens to test the solidity of Atlantic military ties. Even so, the Europeans may be headed for the organization of their own European-based common nuclear defense.

Jerusalem maintains that much of the anguish in its relations with the United States is unnecessary because there is a bedrock mutuality of interest between them. Israelis see U.S. deterrence of direct Soviet intervention, solid military-political support of Israel, and avoidance of confrontation with the USSR as intimately linked. By keeping Soviet forces out of the Arab-Israeli conflict and keeping Israel strong, Washington avoids the necessity of intervening itself. By the same set of actions, Washington also convinces the major Arab states that only the United States holds the key to satisfying their minimum requirements. Thereby it gains room for maneuver without incurring the risks of intervention. In Israeli eyes, it was not so surprising that after the largest U.S. military supply effort to Israel, a U.S. Secretary of State was warmly received in Cairo, more so than on almost any previous occasion.[94]

[94] See the interview with Yitzhak Rabin, in *al Hamishmar,* 16 November 1973.

But in Washington it is believed that Kissinger's welcome in Cairo was made possible by the demonstration of a U.S. commitment to move energetically toward a settlement. Preservation of that momentum, the Nixon Administration feels sure, is the price of continued Egyptian confidence. If the United States holds the key to satisfying minimum Arab demands, it can only be by its capacity to secure Israeli withdrawal. So the circle is joined once more. It will require great dexterity to balance Arab demands, Israeli fears, and the world hunger for oil, without yet another ritual of bloodletting.

The American balancing act also attempts to keep the Soviet-American détente from crashing to the ground. There were differences of opinion in the Western world whether this already occurred in October 1973. Certainly, those who thought as did Douglas-Hume, that "détente is or ought to be the essence of good-neighborliness," found Soviet behavior in the first weeks of October disconcerting. On the eve of the 1972 Moscow summit meetings, Henry Kissinger ventured the opinion that "we are on the verge not just of success in this or that negotiation, but of what could be a new relationship of benefit to all mankind."[95] After the meetings, Kissinger suggested that the Declaration of Basic Principles of Mutual Relations, signed as the capstone of the week's encounters, might signal the end of the race for petty advantage over the other superpower. A world in which such competition continued to be pursued could be too dangerous to live in.[96] The following year, when Brezhnev came to Washington, the sides solemnly agreed "that they will act in such a manner as to prevent the development of situations capable of causing a dnagerous exacerbation of their relations."[97]

Moscow surely knew of the imminence of war in late September and early October but did nothing to forestall the Egyptian-Syrian attack or to alert Washington. When the war came, the Kremlin fanned the flames instead of seeking to damp the fire down—refusing to cooperate in seeking a cease-fire, urging other Arab states to join the battle, and strengthening its client's forces in the midst of the fighting.[98] It did not seem "neighborly" to threaten or hint at unilateral intervention and to engage in alarming maneuvers, such as concentrating airborne forces or appear to be dispatching nuclear materials aboard Soviet ships to Egyptian ports.[99] Communication between the superpowers seemed to consist as much of cold-war techniques—threats, troop movements, alerts—as of the tools of an era of negotiation. Many believed that the Kremlin had chosen

[95] *Newsweek*, 29 May 1972, p.35.
[96] At a news conference in Kiev on May 29: *Department of State Bulletin,* 66 (26 June 1972): 893.
[97] "Agreement on Prevention of Nuclear War Signed June 22," in Department of State, *The Washington Summit: General Secretary Brezhnev's Visit to the United States, June 18–25, 1973* (August 1973), p. 30.
[98] A considerable amount of energy was expended in the United States during the first week of the war debating whether the Soviet airlift was "massive" and if so whether it was "massive enough" to shake the structure of détente.
[99] *The New York Times,* 22 November 1973.

consciously to sacrifice détente for the sake of the gains it believed could be made by exploiting a tempting opportunity in the Middle East.

Washington denied that it had been duped or that détente had crumbled. Instead, it claimed that the existence of détente prevented the transformation of a mini-crisis into a disastrous superpower conflict. The issue, said Kissinger, was not just that a confrontation had taken place (on October 24–25): "But also one has to consider how rapidly the confrontation was ended and how quickly the two sides have attempted to move back to a policy of cooperation in settling the Middle East conflict."[100]   Moscow fully agreed: "The consequences of the military flare-up in the Middle East would undoubtedly have been much more dangerous if the international climate had not thawed and the positive changes in Soviet-U.S. relations had not occurred."[101]

However, the Kremlin saw no contradiction between that defense of the viability of détente and the Soviet role in the Middle East conflict. To the Arabs, Moscow asserted that its stand in October 1973 "completely refutes the main theme of the enemies of Soviet-Arab friendship and cooperation, which says that the détente between the Soviet Union with the United States and other western capitals and countries can affect the Soviet commitments towards its friends and allies. The Soviet Union's speedy and decisive support for the two victims of aggression, Egypt and Syria, dispelled and wiped out this myth."[102]

Soviet support of the other blade of the October scissors, the oil embargo and production cutbacks, was no less solid. Viewing the scramble by Western Europe and Japan to issue pro-Arab statements as pressure from the oil producers increased, Moscow assured the Arab world: "These facts tangibly prove that Arab countries, if unified in their efforts and mobilized in their resources, including the oil weapon, could tighten the noose of international isolation around the neck of the aggressor with greater vigor."[103]   Using a standard technique of citing non-Soviet sources in support of a drastic move, Moscow echoed Arab calls to nationalize American property without compensation. [104] It was suggested that "were the Arab countries to withdraw if only half of their holdings [of foreign exchange in European banks], this would seriously shake the finances of many West European countries."[105]

The war and the exploitation of the "oil weapon" provided the USSR with the opportunity to play on a variety of its propaganda themes, including that of the dangers and weaknesses of the NATO alliance. Italians were warned that their country could have been dragged into war as a result of the extension of the U.S.

[100] *The New York Times,* 22 November 1973, press conference transcript.
[101] P. Demchenko, in *Pravda,* 11 November 1973. See also Kosygin's speech in Minsk, in *Sovetskaia Belorussiia,* 15 November 1973.
[102] Radio Moscow in Arabic, 30 October 1973.
[103] Radio Moscow in Arabic, 5 November 1973.
[104] Radio Peace and Progress in English to Africa, 5 November 1973.
[105] R. Andreasyan, "Middle East: The Oil Factor," *New Times* (no. 45–46, November 1973):18.

alert to American forces in Italy: "Thus, the presence of foreign armed forces on Italian soil has again shown, this time in relation to the Middle East crisis, the serious danger to the country's sovereignty entailed by Italy's membership in NATO."[106] The European states' frantic efforts to assure national supplies of oil and gas evoked the sarcastic comment that "Atlantic solidarity, particularly when it is a question of economic interests, is an entirely ephemeral thing. The oil crisis has shown once more the worth of talk of the 'community of interests' of the western world."[107]

The Middle East war of October 1973 did not shatter the Soviet-American détente, because détente is not in fact "the essence of good-neighborliness." Détente may be a misnomer for the pattern of superpower relations, but whatever name one may choose, the conflict proved the essential stability of that pattern. Kissinger has been at pains to stress that détente did not mean ideological convergence, a theme obviously even more prominent in Soviet apologias for détente. Both sides agree that détente is a condition made inescapable by the nuclear balance of terror. Most likely, the members of the Politburo would agree with the American Secretary of State that the two sides have "a unique relationship." They might also agree with his explication: "We are at one and the same time adversaries and partners in the preservation of peace."[108]

But while the adversary relation is "natural" and almost instinctive, the partnership is wary and derives from the adversaryship itself. It is only because congenital antagonists hold the threat of annihilation over each other's heads that they are led to cooperate in maintaining the peace. Even so, peaceful accommodation is not the sole Soviet method of crisis management. I have attempted to describe a pattern of Soviet behavior in the Middle East that has been characterized by both aggressiveness and circumspection, depending on the circumstances and the perception by both powers of the size of the stakes. The October War provides ample evidence of the continuation of these behavioral propensities.

"The relationship that has developed between the Soviet Union and the United States since 1971," Kissinger suggested after the war, "has been one of considerable restraint."[109] This is a description of the glass half-full. At best, such restraint defines a limited adversary relationship, not a partnership. The Kremlin's public reaffirmations of the necessity for peaceful coexistence reflect no abandonment of the intention to pursue Soviet gains in power competition with the United States. Moscow and Washington became partners in containing the October conflagration only because the U.S. Government resolved to prevent another smashing Israeli victory and Arab defeat. Had the military situation continued to move in the Arabs' favor two weeks after D-day as it did

---

[106] Radio Moscow in Italian, 15 November 1973.
[107] I. Danov, *Sotsialisticheskaia industriia*, 13 November 1973.
[108] *The New York Times*, 26 October 1973.
[109] *The New York Times*, 22 November 1973.

then, the government of the USSR would have seen no reason to stop the fighting. Although Kissinger argued that the crisis of October 24–25 ended quickly because both sides recognized their long-term interests, it was an adversary response that kept the peace that day—U.S. response to the threat of Soviet intervention and the Soviet fear of military confrontation. It is not yet clear that Soviet-American partnership will succeed in bringing a durable settlement to the Middle East.

ACKNOWLEDGMENT: The author wishes to thank Arnold Horelick, Charles Issawi, William Quandt, and Steven Spiegel for their comments and criticisms. Responsibility for the views expressed, of course, remains the author's alone.

Author Index

Page numbers set in italics designate those pages on which the complete literature citation is given.

Numbers in parentheses designate the footnote numbers where information is given.

Subject Index

Entries followed by *n* indicate that information is given in a footnote.

131

Selected Rand Books

Averch, Harvey; Koehler, John E.; and Denton, Frank H. *The Matrix of Policy in the Philippines.* Princeton, N. J.: Princeton University Press, 1971.

Baer, Walter S. *Cable Television: A Handbook for Decisionmaking.* New York: Crane, Russak & Company, 1974.

Becker, Abraham S. *Soviet National Income 1958-1964.* Berkeley and Los Angeles, Calif.: University of California Press, 1969.

Bergson, Abraham S. *The Real National Income of Soviet Russia Since 1928.* Cambridge, Mass.: Harvard University Press, 1961.

Dalkey, Norman, ed. *Studies in the Quality of Life: Delphi and Decisionmaking.* Lexington, Mass.: D. C. Heath, 1972.

Dorfman, Robert; Samuelson, Paul A.; and Solow, Robert M. *Linear Programming and Economic Analysis.* New York: McGraw-Hill, 1958.

Downs, Anthony. *Inside Bureaucracy.* Boston: Little, Brown, 1967.

Einaudi, Luigi R., ed. *Beyond Cuba: Latin America Takes Charge of Its Future.* New York: Crane, Russak & Company, 1974.

Harman, Alvin. *The International Computer Industry: Innovation and Comparative Advantage.* Cambridge, Mass.: Harvard University Press, 1971.

Hirshleifer, Jack; DeHaven, James C.; and Milliman, Jerome W. *Water Supply: Economics, Technology, and Policy.* Chicago, Ill.: University of Chicago Press, 1960.

Hitch, Charles J., and McKean, Roland N. *The Economics of Defense in the Nuclear Age.* Cambridge, Mass.: Harvard University Press, 1960.

Johnson, William A. *The Steel Industry of India.* Cambridge, Mass.: Harvard University Press, 1966.

Johnstone, William C. *Burma's Foreign Policy: A Study in Neutralism.* Cambridge, Mass.: Harvard University Press, 1963.

Leites, Nathan, and Wolf, Charles Jr. *Rebellion and Authority.* Chicago, Ill.: Markham, 1970.

Liu, Ta-Chung, and Yeh, Kung-Chia. *The Economy of the Chinese Mainland: National Income and Economic Development, 1933-1959.* Princeton, N.J.: Princeton University Press, 1965.

Lubell, Harold. *Middle East Oil Crises and Western Europe's Energy Supplies.* Baltimore, M.: The Johns Hopkins University Press, 1963.

Marschak, Thomas; Glennan, Jr., Thomas K.; and Summers, Robert. *Strategy for R&D.* New York: Springer-Verlag, 1967.

McCall, John J. *Income Mobility, Racial Discrimination, and Economic Growth.* Lexington, Mass.: D. C. Heath, 1973.

McKean, Roland N. *Efficiency in Government Through Systems Analysis: With Emphasis on Water Resource Development.* New York: John Wiley, 1958.

Nelson, Richard R.; Peck, Merton J.; and Kalachek, Edward D. *Technology Economic Growth and Public Policy.* Washington, D.C.: The Brookings Institution, 1967.

Nelson, Richard R.; Slighton, Robert L.; and Schultz, T. Paul. *Structural Change in a Developing Economy: Columbia's Problems and Prospects.* Princeton, N. J.: Princeton University Press, 1971.

Newhouse, Joseph P., and Alexander, Arthur J. *An Economic Analysis of Public Library Services.* Lexington, Mass.: D. C. Heath 1972.

Park, Rolla Edward. *The Role of Analysis in Regulatory Decisionmaking.* Lexington, Mass.: D. C. Heath, 1973.

Pascal, Anthony. *Thinking About Cities: New Perspectives on Urban Problems.* Belmont, Calif.: Dickenson, 1970.

Phillips, Almarin, *Technology and Market Structure: A Study of the Aircraft Industry.* Lexington, Mass.: D. C. Heath Company, 1971.

Quandt, William B., ed. *The Politics of Palestinian Nationalism.* Calif.: University of California Press, 1973.

Rosen, George. *Democracy and Economic Change in India.* Berkeley and Los Angeles, Calif.: University of California Press, 1966.

Stepan, Alfred. *The Military in Politics: Changing Patterns in Brazil.* Princeton, N. J.: Princeton University Press, 1971.

Wolf, Charles, Jr. *Foreign Aid: Theory and Practice in Southern Asia.* Princeton, N. J.: Princeton University Press, 1960.